LESSONS *from*
LEGENDS

*Powerful Life Principles
from Thirteen Compelling Bible Characters*

MARK RASMUSSEN

Copyright © 2011 by Striving Together Publications. All Scripture quotations are taken from the King James Version.

First published in 2011 by Striving Together Publications, a ministry of Lancaster Baptist Church, Lancaster, CA 93535. Striving Together Publications is committed to providing tried, trusted, and proven books that will further equip local churches to carry out the Great Commission. Your comments and suggestions are valued.

All rights reserved. No part of this book may be reproduced, stored in a retrieval system, or transmitted in any form or by any means— electronic, mechanical, photocopy, recording, or otherwise—without written permission of the publisher, except for brief quotations in printed reviews.

Striving Together Publications
4020 E. Lancaster Blvd.
Lancaster, CA 93535
800.201.7748

Cover design by Andrew Jones
Layout by Craig Parker
Edited by David Coon
Special thanks to our proofreaders.

ISBN 978-1-59894-167-8

Printed in the United States of America

TABLE OF CONTENTS

Why Use Sunday School Curriculum? v

How to Use This Curriculum ix

Lesson One   Joshua. 1
Training for Leadership

Lesson Two   Caleb 19
Mountain Claiming

Lesson Three   Barnabas 35
The Encourager

Lesson Four   John. 51
The Beloved

Lesson Five   Jeremiah 65
Heart of Compassion

Lesson Six   Ruth... 79
From Defeat to Victory

Lesson Seven   Job 97
Trusting in Tribulations

Lesson Eight   Samson 111
Wasted Potential

Lesson Nine   Centurion 125
The Man Who Amazed Jesus

Lesson Ten   Esther. 143
Found Faithful

Lesson Eleven   Elisha 157
A Double Portion

Lesson Twelve   Joseph. .173
Living Like Jesus

Lesson Thirteen   Jonathan 189
True Friendship

WHY USE SUNDAY SCHOOL CURRICULUM?

Are there some really compelling reasons to use a Sunday school curriculum? We believe YES! For nearly two-and-a-half decades, God has developed strong Christians at Lancaster Baptist Church, and a huge part of that process is the Adult Bible Class Ministry and curriculum. Several years ago, through *Striving Together Publications*, we made a serious commitment to produce curricula for local church ministries. Here are five solid reasons to use curricula with student books:

1.   Equip the Teacher

While many teachers are gifted at organizing material into memorable outlines and thought flow, many are not. There's nothing worse than listening to good Bible material put through an "impossible to follow" thought flow! Most teachers appreciate having a basic outline of biblical material to use as a launching pad—a starting point and guideline. Guaranteed—providing a

v

solid series of outlines for your teachers is an investment that will reap a huge harvest in your adult class ministry.

2. Engage the Students

When you place a student book into the hands of your students, you say something very valuable. You are saying, "We are interested in making a serious investment into your spiritual growth." You say, "Take this class seriously." You say, "Come back next week for the next lesson in this series." You say, "We are preparing every week to build your Christian life." These are powerful messages that make the minor cost of a student book well worth it.

3. Establish Commitment

Using a series of lessons builds continuity from week to week that encourages students to commit to a class. It lets them know they are missing something if they don't return. This is effective for regular attenders as well as first-time visitors. Think of the impact on visitors when they walk into a class, receive a warm welcome, and are then handed a student book for the present series.

4. Encourage Follow Up Study

Using the student books provides the class members with a weekly assignment including review questions for discussion or personal devotions. This also provides the teacher some thoughts for opening discussion each week and reviewing the previous lesson.

5. Enable a Journey of Spiritual Growth

Using student books gives each class member a growing library that chronicles their own growth. Let's face it, weekly photocopies end up in the trash. But few people would ever throw away a student book. They will save them and be able to look back over them in the years to come—that's valuable.

In spite of these great reasons, many still wrestle with three common obstacles to using curriculum:

1.   What about cost?

The most common question we receive about *Striving Together* curriculum is, "Can we photocopy the lesson for our students?" The answer is always "no." Why?

First, it's just a bad practice. The students will throw away the photocopies. They won't save them. So your time, your money, your copier is all wasted—bad stewardship.

Second, we couldn't continue providing curriculum if that practice continued.

Third, we believe strongly in the value of a student guide— it is much greater than the cost. *Striving Together* student guides can be purchased for as little as $2 and $3. In most cases, this is more cost effective than photocopying when you account for the paper, time, labor, and copier costs. On top of that, the five-point list above is worth far more than a few dollars in the life of every growing Christian.

2.   Do the students really use it?

The simple answer is, "yes and no." Most do, some don't. Frankly, you'll probably never get an entire class to use the student books in their entirety. The point is, many will! And many others will use them partially. The class may require some reminding. You may end up providing replacements for a few lost books along the way. You may have folks who miss a few lessons. But ultimately, most of your class will use the books and benefit from them. Over time, you will build the habit and expectation into the DNA of your Sunday school. And that's worth working toward.

vii

3. Is it really that effective?

Yes. Look at the five things above and ask yourself if you would like to see these things in your adult and youth classes. Sunday school curriculum will improve your teachers and engage your students at a whole new level. It's an investment you can't afford not to make.

Striving Together curriculum is often designed to provide the teacher with more material than can be taught in thirteen weeks. That's on purpose. We want to provide plenty of good content in every resource. The sooner you begin making this investment, the sooner it will start to pay back on multiple levels.

Sunday school curriculum is a great way to take your adult and youth classes to the next level.

HOW TO USE THIS CURRICULUM

Take a moment to familiarize yourself with the features of this *Striving Together* Sunday school curriculum:

Schedule

The lessons contained in this curriculum are undated, allowing you to begin and end the teaching series at any time. There are thirteen lessons that may be taught weekly any time of the year.

Student Edition Books

Companion books are available through *Striving Together Publications.* These contain:

- The outlines with blanks that students may fill in during the lessons
- Various Scripture quotations that are used throughout each lesson

- The introductory lesson overviews
- Study questions for review throughout the week
- A suggested memory verse for each lesson

These books are excellent tools for the members of a class. We suggest ordering enough books for each member of the class, plus additional copies for new members who enroll in the class throughout the teaching series. Giving class members a study book encourages faithfulness to the class, provides students with a devotional tool for use throughout the week, and allows them to review what they learned previously.

Text

The verses from which the lessons are taken are included at the beginning of each lesson. These are provided so that you may read them through several times in prayerful preparation for your time in class. Many teachers choose to memorize their text. During the class hour, we suggest that you use your own Bible for Scripture reading and encourage your class members to do so as well.

Overview and Lesson Aim

The summary and aim sections are provided so that you may be aware of the overall emphasis of each lesson, especially as they relate to the other lessons in the curriculum. These brief statements provide a snapshot of where each lesson will take your students.

Lesson Goals

Bible teaching has a higher goal than the delivery of information. That goal is a changed life. Students want to know what they are to do with what they are given from God's Word. As you prepare for and teach each lesson, emphasize how those listening may apply its truths throughout the week.

Teaching Outline

The abbreviated outline enables you to view the entire lesson at a glance to see how the content fits together. Teaching with an organized outline increases the students' abilities to understand and remember the lesson content.

LESSON ONE

JOSHUA
Training for Leadership

Text

JOSHUA 1:1–8

1   Now after the death of Moses the servant of the LORD it came to pass, that the LORD spake unto Joshua the son of Nun, Moses' minister, saying,

2   Moses my servant is dead; now therefore arise, go over this Jordan, thou, and all this people, unto the land which I do give to them, even to the children of Israel.

3   Every place that the sole of your foot shall tread upon, that have I given unto you, as I said unto Moses.

4   From the wilderness and this Lebanon even unto the great river, the river Euphrates, all the land of the Hittites, and unto the great sea toward the going down of the sun, shall be your coast.

5   There shall not any man be able to stand before thee all the days of thy life: as I was with Moses, so I will be with thee: I will not fail thee, nor forsake thee.

6   Be strong and of a good courage: for unto this people shalt thou divide for an inheritance the land, which I sware unto their fathers to give them.

7   Only be thou strong and very courageous, that thou mayest observe to do according to all the law, which Moses my servant commanded thee: turn not from it to the right hand or to the left, that thou mayest prosper whithersoever thou goest.

8   This book of the law shall not depart out of thy mouth; but thou shalt meditate therein day and night, that thou mayest observe to do according to all that is written therein: for then thou shalt make thy way prosperous, and then thou shalt have good success.

Overview

Much of our learning comes through the power of examples. Therefore, the wise Christian will deliberately find godly

1

examples and follow them. In Joshua we see a man who spent years in preparation under a great leader, and so became fit to become the leader himself in God's own time.

Lesson Theme

We think of Joshua as a great warrior, whose power and success were due to the blessing of God on his life. At the same time, it is important for us to see that Joshua was a trained and prepared man as well. God used Joshua's time of training under Moses to prepare him for the leadership of the nation. If we will take the time and effort to become prepared, God will be able to use us more effectively as well.

Lesson Goals

At the conclusion of this lesson, students should:

1. Know the basic facts of the life of Joshua
2. Understand the importance of Joshua's training and preparation
3. Choose to be both patient under training and diligent in preparation

Teaching Outline

Introduction

   I. Serving the Saint
     A. Faithful to follow
     B. Faithful to fight

  II. Seeking the Sovereign
     A. Will
     B. Direction

 III. Conquering a Country
     A. The land was dangerous.
     B. The Lord was victorious.

Conclusion

LESSON ONE

JOSHUA
Training for Leadership

Text

JOSHUA 1:1–8

1   Now after the death of Moses the servant of the LORD it came to pass, that the LORD spake unto Joshua the son of Nun, Moses' minister, saying,

2   Moses my servant is dead; now therefore arise, go over this Jordan, thou, and all this people, unto the land which I do give to them, even to the children of Israel.

3   Every place that the sole of your foot shall tread upon, that have I given unto you, as I said unto Moses.

4   From the wilderness and this Lebanon even unto the great river, the river Euphrates, all the land of the Hittites, and unto the great sea toward the going down of the sun, shall be your coast.

5   There shall not any man be able to stand before thee all the days of thy life: as I was with Moses, so I will be with thee: I will not fail thee, nor forsake thee.

6   Be strong and of a good courage: for unto this people shalt thou divide for an inheritance the land, which I sware unto their fathers to give them.

7   Only be thou strong and very courageous, that thou mayest observe to do according to all the law, which Moses my servant commanded thee: turn not from it to the right hand or to the left, that thou mayest prosper whithersoever thou goest.

8   This book of the law shall not depart out of thy mouth; but thou shalt meditate therein day and night, that thou mayest observe to do according to all that is written therein: for then thou shalt make thy way prosperous, and then thou shalt have good success.

Introduction

It is a wonderful thing when a great leader is succeeded by someone who continues to take the work forward effectively. Such was the case for Moses. God's promises to the Israelites and to Moses were ultimately fulfilled because God's man did God's work in God's way. Today, we will see how Joshua was trained and how he put that training into action in his life. The principles that we see in Joshua's life are certainly applicable to those who seek to have God use them today.

I.   Serving the <u>Saint</u>

JOSHUA 1:1

*1   Now after the death of Moses the servant of the LORD it came to pass, that the LORD spake unto Joshua the son of Nun, **Moses' minister**, saying…*

As has been the case with so many other men whom God has used, Joshua first showed a willingness to be a servant before becoming a sovereign. Unfortunately today, whether in the realm of politics, athletics, or church work, the step of servanthood is something that many attempt to disparage, get through quickly with the least effort possible, or bypass altogether. There is something to be said for one who has spent time in the trenches, whether the "trenches" be changing diapers in the nursery, baking

4

Lesson One—Joshua—Training for Leadership

for dozens in the kitchen, or being broiled by the sun while directing cars and people safely through a parking lot. It has been said that the only place success comes before work is in the dictionary!

Illustration (good followers are hard to find, *None of These Diseases*, S.I. McMillen)

S. I. McMillen, in his book *None of These Diseases* tells a story of a young woman who wanted to go to college, but her heart sank when she read the question on the application blank that asked, "Are you a leader?" Being both honest and conscientious, she wrote, "No," and returned the application, expecting the worst. To her surprise, she received this letter from the college: "Dear Applicant: A study of the application forms reveals that this year our college will have 1,452 new leaders. We are accepting you because we feel it is imperative that they have at least one follower."

Illustration (service before success, Dave Thomas)

Dave Thomas, the founder of Wendy's Restaurants, who died a few years ago, became a familiar sight to millions in his company's television commercials. Dave also appeared in a lot of in-store training films. In those, as in many of the more familiar commercials, he would dress as his workers. One year he appeared on the cover of one of the company's annual reports dressed in a knee-length work apron holding a mop and a plastic bucket. For many years, a framed copy of that picture graced the back rooms and managers' offices of most Wendy's. That picture was built on the fact that Dave was a self-made millionaire. He didn't finish high school. He worked his way up through the ranks of Colonel Sanders' Kentucky Fried Chicken chain long before he went off on his own and started Wendy's. Here's how Dave explained that picture: "I got my M.B.A. long before my G.E.D. At Wendy's, M.B.A. does not mean Master of Business Administration: It means Mop Bucket Attitude." Dave Thomas taught all of his employees that service comes before success. (Dr. Roger W. Thomas, http://www.witandwisdom.org)

A. Faithful to follow

Exodus 24:13–14

13 *And Moses rose up, and his minister Joshua: and Moses went up into the mount of God.*

14 *And he said unto the elders, Tarry ye here for us, until we come again unto you: and, behold, Aaron and Hur are with you: if any man have any matters to do, let him come unto them.*

Exodus 32:15–17

15 *And Moses turned, and went down from the mount, and the two tables of the testimony were in his hand: the tables were written on both their sides; on the one side and on the other were they written.*

16 *And the tables were the work of God, and the writing was the writing of God, graven upon the tables.*

17 *And when Joshua heard the noise of the people as they shouted, he said unto Moses, There is a noise of war in the camp.*

Joshua gives us a classic illustration of someone who faithfully followed his leader, even when Joshua did not know where the leader was or what the leader was doing. Moses, the leader and mentor, had taken Joshua with him to Mount Carmel—where he then "disappeared" for over a month. Joshua, however, did not desert the post where his leader had seemingly abandoned him. Rather, Joshua was steadfast, steady, and submissive to the wishes of his leader. Dr. Bobby Roberson has said that the one thing that everyone can do is to "be in their place." This was the case with Joshua. When Moses descended with the Ten Commandments in his hand, Joshua was right in his place—the same place to which Moses had assigned him weeks earlier.

Illustration (loyalty to the leader)

Robert E. Lee said of Stonewall Jackson, "Such an executive officer the sun never shone on. I have but to show him my design, and I know that if it can be done it will be done. No need for me to send or watch him. Straight as the needle to

Lesson One—Joshua—Training for Leadership

the pole he advances to the execution of my purpose." (Hon. Francis Lawley in the London *Times*, June 16, 1863, quoted in *Stonewall Jackson And The American Civil War* by G. F. R. Henderson)

B. FAITHFUL TO FIGHT

EXODUS 17:8–13

8   Then came Amalek, and fought with Israel in Rephidim.

9   **And Moses said unto Joshua, Choose us out men, and go out, fight with Amalek:** to morrow I will stand on the top of the hill with the rod of God in mine hand.

10   So Joshua did as Moses had said to him, and fought with Amalek: and Moses, Aaron, and Hur went up to the top of the hill.

11   And it came to pass, when Moses held up his hand, that Israel prevailed: and when he let down his hand, Amalek prevailed.

12   But Moses' hands were heavy; and they took a stone, and put it under him, and he sat thereon; and Aaron and Hur stayed up his hands, the one on the one side, and the other on the other side; and his hands were steady until the going down of the sun.

13   And Joshua discomfited Amalek and his people with the edge of the sword.

If one were to attempt to describe Joshua, most would probably say that he was a great general. It is said that the tactics of Joshua have been studied by many students of the science of war at many prestigious places such as West Point Military Academy. Several times Joshua was commanded by Moses to fight, and we never see him dissent or balk at the orders of his leader. He was willing to follow God's man and enter into disagreeable and dangerous situations, even when this placed him in great personal peril.

The Christian life is called "warfare" for a good reason. One characteristic that is inevitably tied to being a soldier is a willingness to fight. The famous reformer Martin Luther said, "Where the battle rages is where the loyalty of the soldier is proved...."

Joshua conquered thirty-one kings and ten cities in his military career. God's men have continually been willing to go into conflict—as David did at the valley of Elah, while his brothers and their fellow soldiers stood by with their proverbial hands in their pockets. The Christian is faced with the choice of being either a spectator or a participant in the battle. The hymn-writer William Sherwin, who wrote "Sound the Battle Cry," captured the Christian warrior's spirit perfectly when he said, "Sound the battle cry! See, the foe is nigh. Raise the standard high for the Lord...."

Illustration (loyalty to death)

When asked to renounce his loyalty to the king or lose his head on the chopping block, the Scottish Marquis of Huntly responded resolutely, "You can take my head from my shoulders, but you will never take my heart from my king." That has been the testimony of many followers of Christ in a multitude of situations over the centuries. (Rev. King Duncan, Dynamic Preaching)

II. Seeking the <u>Sovereign</u>

JOSHUA 1:2–5

2   *Moses my servant is dead; now therefore arise, go over this Jordan, thou, and all this people, unto the land which I do give to them, even to the children of Israel.*

3   *Every place that the sole of your foot shall tread upon, that have I given unto you, as I said unto Moses.*

4   *From the wilderness and this Lebanon even unto the great river, the river Euphrates, all the land of the Hittites, and unto the great sea toward the going down of the sun, shall be your coast.*

5   *There shall not any man be able to stand before thee all the days of thy life: **as I was with Moses, so I will be with thee: I will not fail thee, nor forsake thee.***

Lesson One—Joshua—Training for Leadership

In preparation for leadership, we find that Joshua was totally in tune with the desires and wishes of the man whom God had placed over him. While we think of Moses as one of God's all-time great men, it would be appropriate to realize that to Joshua, he was simply "boss."

A. WILL

NUMBERS 14:6–9

6 *And Joshua the son of Nun, and Caleb the son of Jephunneh, which were of them that searched the land, rent their clothes:*

7 *And they spake unto all the company of the children of Israel, saying, The land, which we passed through to search it, is an exceeding good land.*

8 ***If the LORD delight in us, then he will bring us into this land, and give it us;*** *a land which floweth with milk and honey.*

9 ***Only rebel not ye against the LORD,*** *neither fear ye the people of the land; for they are bread for us: their defence is departed from them, and the LORD is with us: fear them not.*

One of Joshua's first important jobs was that of being a spy charged with infiltrating and reporting on the land that was promised to Israel. Joshua accepted the responsibility of this daunting task—a responsibility of which only twelve men from the entire nation of Israel were deemed worthy. Joshua accepted that God's will could and would be done. Although in a clear minority, he returned from his expedition of espionage believing that God would enable His people to take the land. We need people today who, though in a minority, believe that God **can**, but more importantly, believe that He **will** accomplish His purpose.

B. DIRECTION

JOSHUA 5:13–6:5

13 *And it came to pass, when Joshua was by Jericho, that he lifted up his eyes and looked, and, behold, there stood a man over against him with his sword drawn in his hand: and*

9

Joshua went unto him, and said unto him, Art thou for us, or for our adversaries?

14 And he said, Nay; but as captain of the host of the LORD am I now come. And Joshua fell on his face to the earth, and did worship, and said unto him, What saith my lord unto his servant?

15 And the captain of the LORD's host said unto Joshua, Loose thy shoe from off thy foot; for the place whereon thou standest is holy. And Joshua did so.

6:1 Now Jericho was straitly shut up because of the children of Israel: none went out, and none came in.

2 And the LORD said unto Joshua, See, I have given into thine hand Jericho, and the king thereof, and the mighty men of valour.

3 And ye shall compass the city, all ye men of war, and go round about the city once. Thus shalt thou do six days.

4 And seven priests shall bear before the ark seven trumpets of rams' horns: and the seventh day ye shall compass the city seven times, and the priests shall blow with the trumpets.

5 And it shall come to pass, that when they make a long blast with the ram's horn, and when ye hear the sound of the trumpet, all the people shall shout with a great shout; and the wall of the city shall fall down flat, and the people shall ascend up every man straight before him.

Joshua 8:1–7

1 And the LORD said unto Joshua, Fear not, neither be thou dismayed: take all the people of war with thee, and arise, go up to Ai: see, I have given into thy hand the king of Ai, and his people, and his city, and his land:

2 And thou shalt do to Ai and her king as thou didst unto Jericho and her king: only the spoil thereof, and the cattle thereof, shall ye take for a prey unto yourselves: lay thee an ambush for the city behind it.

3 So Joshua arose, and all the people of war, to go up against Ai: and Joshua chose out thirty thousand mighty men of valour, and sent them away by night.

4 And he commanded them, saying, Behold, ye shall lie in wait against the city, even behind the city: go not very far from the city, but be ye all ready:

Lesson One—Joshua—Training for Leadership

5   And I, and all the people that are with me, will approach unto the city: and it shall come to pass, when they come out against us, as at the first, that we will flee before them,

6   (For they will come out after us) till we have drawn them from the city; for they will say, They flee before us, as at the first: therefore we will flee before them.

7   Then ye shall rise up from the ambush, and seize upon the city: for the LORD your God will deliver it into your hand.

Like many great leaders in the Bible, Joshua was not faultless and did suffer defeat. The battle of Ai resulted in a crushing defeat at the hands of an inferior foe. Israel had sin in the camp and Joshua had not sought God's direction about his next move. Although they marched confidently into battle, the Israelites were routed. After the defeat, Joshua sought the face of the Lord, and God revealed to him first the means of discovering the guilty party and then the means of defeating Ai. When Joshua faithfully followed God's directions, the guilty one was found out and the victory was won.

This was not the first time that Joshua had followed the direction of the Lord even when common sense would have led him to act otherwise. While planning the attack on the city of Jericho, Joshua was visited by the captain of the host of the LORD who delivered quite unusual plans for dealing with Jericho. However, when Joshua did God's work in God's way, God gave him the victory.

Illustration

Once there were two young men who were planning the details of a city-wide crusade. What speaker should they invite to come and declare the Word of God to them? Who would be the best choice? One strongly declared his desire to see Dwight L. Moody lead the revival and pushed for him to be the speaker. The other tartly asked him, "Do you think Moody has a monopoly on God?" The man replied, "No, but I believe God has a monopoly on Moody."

III. Conquering a **Country**

JOSHUA 1:6–8

6   Be strong and of a good courage: for unto this people shalt thou divide for an inheritance the land, which I sware unto their fathers to give them.

7   Only be thou strong and very courageous, that thou mayest observe to do according to all the law, which Moses my servant commanded thee: turn not from it to the right hand or to the left, that thou mayest prosper whithersoever thou goest.

8   This book of the law shall not depart out of thy mouth; but thou shalt meditate therein day and night, that thou mayest observe to do according to all that is written therein: for then thou shalt make thy way prosperous, and then thou shalt have good success.

The church of the living God is to be on the offensive. God's Word says that the gates of Hell will not prevail against His church. Through God's enablement, there can be victory over the world, the flesh, and the devil. As surely as Joshua fought against the Amalekites, Perizzites, Amorites, and others, Christians today will be involved in a continual spiritual warfare until the return of the Lord Jesus Christ. And just as the victory was promised to Joshua, there is a sure outcome for our current war. We simply must decide to give our all in the fight.

Illustration (resolution, quote—Winston Churchill, speech to the House of Commons after Dunkirk, June 4, 1940)
Prospects looked very grim for England in June of 1940. Hitler's German armies had overrun most of continental Europe and had driven the British forces to the coast of France. With the intervention of God and the valiant efforts of the entire British nation, well over 300,000 soldiers were rescued from the beaches of Dunkirk. But as the British Prime Minister Winston Churchill noted, "Wars are not won by evacuations." Now Britain stood virtually alone against the threatened Nazi invasion of their home island. But Churchill refused to be intimidated, as he assured his people: "…we shall not flag or fail. We shall go on to the end; we

Lesson One—Joshua—Training for Leadership

shall fight in France; we shall fight on the seas and oceans; we shall fight with growing confidence and growing strength in the air; we shall defend our island. Whatever the cost may be, we shall fight on the beaches; we shall fight on the landing grounds; we shall fight in the fields and in the streets; we shall fight in the hills. We shall never surrender...."

A. THE LAND WAS DANGEROUS.

NUMBERS 13:31–33

31 But the men that went up with him said, We be not able to go up against the people; for they are stronger than we.

32 And they brought up an evil report of the land which they had searched unto the children of Israel, saying, The land, through which we have gone to search it, is a land that eateth up the inhabitants thereof; and all the people that we saw in it are men of a great stature.

33 And there we saw the giants, the sons of Anak, which come of the giants: and we were in our own sight as grasshoppers, and so we were in their sight.

In understanding the dangers of the land the spies explored, there is really only one word that needs to be spoken...GIANTS! The problems that Christians face will not always be little problems. Sometimes, there are big problems, but no matter what the size of our problems, we can be sure that we are on the winning side. Problems that can be hurled at the believer today could be connected with family, finances, physical health, or any number of things. When dangers arise, they should not bring shock or surprise, but rather, they should spur God's people to a renewed dependence upon the Lord.

B. THE LORD WAS VICTORIOUS.

JOSHUA 6:7

7 And he said unto the people, Pass on, and compass the city, and let him that is armed pass on before the ark of the LORD.

Joshua 6:20

*20 So the people shouted when the priests blew with the trumpets: and it came to pass, when the people heard the sound of the trumpet, and the people shouted with a great shout, that the wall fell down flat, so that the people went up into the city, every man straight before him, **and they took the city**.*

God has victories for His people today that He is simply waiting for them to claim. There is no doubt that Joshua went forward to claim the victory because he firmly believed in his heart the promises of God. One song writer said it this way, "Every promise in the book is mine, every chapter, every verse, every line."

While it is true that every knee will one day bow and every tongue will confess that Jesus Christ is Lord, it is equally true that victories can be claimed and won in the Christian life today.

Illustration (David Livingstone, First White Man to Walk across Africa)

Buried today in Westminster Abbey is a man who dared to go where no missionary had ever before trodden. The dangers were innumerable: he traveled thousands of miles on foot; he was mauled and crippled by a lion; his body was wracked by such debilitating diseases as malaria and dysentery. While he is famous for his explorations of the African interior and the discovery of Victoria Falls, for the natives of Africa he did something far more important: he brought to them the knowledge of the Lord Jesus Christ. The great missionary pioneer David Livingstone died as he communicated with the Lord from his knees; while his body was carried one thousand miles to the African coast to be sent back to England, his heart was removed and buried in Africa, for the Africans declared, "His heart belongs to us."

Lesson One—Joshua—Training for Leadership

Conclusion

As believers, we can follow in the steps of Joshua in three ways: First, we need to make sure we follow the spiritual leaders whom God places in our lives. Next, we should seek to find God's will for our lives and walk in it. Finally, we must do our best to focus not on the challenges before us, but rather on the power of God in order that we might win victories for the cause of Christ. How are you doing?

Lessons from Legends

Study Questions

1. Who was the man Joshua followed? List some examples of Joshua's "follow-ship."
    Joshua followed Moses. Joshua was faithful to stay at the foot of the mountain while Moses stayed with God for forty days receiving the commandments. Joshua carried out the orders of Moses in the battle with the Amalekites.

2. Finish this thought: Before one can expect to become a leader, he or she must first spend time as a _____.
    servant

3. Describe Joshua's first expedition into the Promised Land.
    He was one of the twelve spies sent in by Moses, and he was one of the two who believed that God would give them the land.

4. Where did Joshua get his encouragement and his battle plan for the conquest of Jericho?
    The captain of the host of the Lord told him what to do and how to do it.

5. Where and why did Joshua meet his greatest defeat?
    Joshua and the Israelites were defeated in the battle of Ai, because there was sin in the camp of Israel and Joshua had failed to seek God's direction and blessing.

6. How should you react to the inevitable problems and even dangers that come as you seek to serve God?
    Answers will vary but could include the following: courage, faith, dependence upon God.

Lesson One—Joshua—Training for Leadership

7. What was the basis of Joshua's firm belief that the victory would be won?
    He knew and trusted the promises of God.

8. What are some practical ways in which we can follow the steps of Joshua?
    Answers will vary but could include the following: follow the leaders God has given us, always seek God's direction in our lives, believe what God has said and act on it.

Memory Verse

This book of the law shall not depart out of thy mouth; but thou shalt meditate therein day and night, that thou mayest observe to do according to all that is written therein: for then thou shalt make thy way prosperous, and then thou shalt have good success.
—JOSHUA 1:8

LESSON TWO

CALEB
Mountain Claiming

Text

JOSHUA 14:6–12

6   Then the children of Judah came unto Joshua in Gilgal: and Caleb the son of Jephunneh the Kenezite said unto him, Thou knowest the thing that the LORD said unto Moses the man of God concerning me and thee in Kadeshbarnea.

7   Forty years old was I when Moses the servant of the LORD sent me from Kadeshbarnea to espy out the land; and I brought him word again as it was in mine heart.

8   Nevertheless my brethren that went up with me made the heart of the people melt: but I wholly followed the LORD my God.

9   And Moses sware on that day, saying, Surely the land whereon thy feet have trodden shall be thine inheritance, and thy children's for ever, because thou hast wholly followed the LORD my God.

10   And now, behold, the LORD hath kept me alive, as he said, these forty and five years, even since the LORD spake this word unto Moses, while the children of Israel wandered in the wilderness: and now, lo, I am this day fourscore and five years old.

11   As yet I am as strong this day as I was in the day that Moses sent me: as my strength was then, even so is my strength now, for war, both to go out, and to come in.

12   Now therefore give me this mountain, whereof the LORD spake in that day; for thou heardest in that day how the Anakims were there, and that the cities were great and fenced: if so be the LORD will be with me, then I shall be able to drive them out, as the LORD said.

Overview

In Caleb we see an example of a faithful man who first believed the promise of God, then trusted Him through forty-five years of good times and bad times, and finally claimed that promise for the glory of God.

Lesson Theme

Caleb wanted his mountain, but he was willing to wait for decades to claim the promise of God and to achieve his goal in God's time and God's way. We, too, need to believe God enough to trust that His way is always best and that He will do the right thing at exactly the right time.

Lesson Goals

At the conclusion of the lesson, each student should:

1. Understand the importance of knowing the Word of God
2. Understand the importance of a spirit that is submissive to God
3. Determine to conduct his life according to God's ways and God's timing

Teaching Outline

Introduction

    I. Relied on God
       A. As a follower
       B. As a leader

    II. Remained Faithful
       A. Attitude
       B. Obedience

    III. Remembered the Promises
       A. The promise of the land
       B. The promise of the victory
       C. The promise of the age

Conclusion

LESSON TWO

CALEB
Mountain Claiming

Text

JOSHUA 14:6–12

6   Then the children of Judah came unto Joshua in Gilgal: and Caleb the son of Jephunneh the Kenezite said unto him, Thou knowest the thing that the LORD said unto Moses the man of God concerning me and thee in Kadeshbarnea.

7   Forty years old was I when Moses the servant of the LORD sent me from Kadeshbarnea to espy out the land; and I brought him word again as it was in mine heart.

8   Nevertheless my brethren that went up with me made the heart of the people melt: but I wholly followed the LORD my God.

9   And Moses sware on that day, saying, Surely the land whereon thy feet have trodden shall be thine inheritance, and thy children's for ever, because thou hast wholly followed the LORD my God.

10   And now, behold, the LORD hath kept me alive, as he said, these forty and five years, even since the LORD spake this word unto Moses, while the children of Israel wandered in the wilderness: and now, lo, I am this day fourscore and five years old.

11   As yet I am as strong this day as I was in the day that Moses sent me: as my strength was then, even so is my strength now, for war, both to go out, and to come in.

12   Now therefore give me this mountain, whereof the LORD spake in that day; for thou heardest in that day how the Anakims were there, and that the cities were great and fenced: if so be the LORD will be with me, then I shall be able to drive them out, as the LORD said.

Introduction

While the Christian life is undoubtedly a series of peaks and valleys, it is, above all, to be an upward journey. This truth is beautifully pictured by John Bunyan's allegorical story *Pilgrim's Progress* in which he describes the lead character, Christian, as one who is continually struggling upward toward the goal of the Celestial City.

The church today needs people who will leave the valley and climb the mountains of opportunity that God places into their paths. Edmund Hillary, the first to successfully climb Mt. Everest, was asked why he attempted to climb the highest mountain in the world. His answer was that there are some views that are only accessible at the very top. As Christians today, we often find ourselves plodding in the valley when the Lord's desire for us is to attain the opportunities that are only available at the top of the mountains.

I.   Relied on <u>God</u>

One of the most important aspects of Caleb's life is that he knew what God said, and because of his understanding of God's words, he was able to exhort others with those truths that God had given. We, too, need to be aware of the words of God, and to be aware that God's Word is pure, powerful, and precise. It is, if you will, our GPS for life. Like Caleb, we need to know God's Word so that we may faithfully obey it.

Illustration

Even the Lord Jesus Himself used Scripture to stand up to the temptations of Satan. In Matthew 4 and Luke 4, we see the replies Christ made to each of the temptations:

To the temptation of the lust of the flesh, Jesus said, "It is written, That man shall not live by bread alone, but by every word of God" (Luke 4:4).

To the temptation of the lust of the eyes, Jesus said, "Get thee behind me, Satan: for it is written, Thou shalt worship the Lord thy God, and him only shalt thou serve" (Luke 4:8).

To the temptation of the lust of the pride of life, Jesus said, "It is said, Thou shalt not tempt the Lord thy God" (Luke 4:12).

Illustration (knowing God's Word and following it)

King David's view of Scripture from Psalm 119:

11 *Thy word have I hid in mine heart, that I might not sin against thee.*

105 *Thy word is a lamp unto my feet, and a light unto my path.*

Illustration

For Ezra had prepared his heart to seek the law of the LORD, and to do it, and to teach in Israel statutes and judgments.—EZRA 7:10

God wants us to seek His Word; He wants us to learn His Word. We cannot truly obey the Bible and teach the Bible until we first know the Bible in a real and personal way. Psalm 119:11 gives us an example to follow: "Thy word have I hid in mine heart, that I might not sin against thee." God wants us to hide His Word in our hearts. The heart is the seat of our emotions and our actions, so we must allow God's Word to penetrate our hearts and thus permeate our lives. Proverbs 4:23 tells us to "Keep thy heart with all diligence; for out of it are the issues of life." The quality of our lives is determined by the quality of our hearts, and that is why we need to hide God's Word in our hearts. God wants us to seek His Word as Ezra did, and to learn it thoroughly.

Even when Caleb conquered his mountain, he did it God's way and in God's timing. There is no doubt that Caleb would have preferred to go into the Promised Land and take his inheritance long before he did, but he allowed God to guide him and he faithfully followed that guidance.

A. As a FOLLOWER

JOSHUA 14:6–8

6 *Then the children of Judah came unto Joshua in Gilgal: and Caleb the son of Jephunneh the Kenezite said unto him, Thou knowest the thing that the LORD said unto Moses the man of God concerning me and thee in Kadesh-barnea.*

7 *Forty years old was I when Moses the servant of the LORD sent me from Kadesh-barnea to espy out the land; and I brought him word again as it was in mine heart.*

8 *Nevertheless my brethren that went up with me made the heart of the people melt: **but I wholly followed the LORD my God.***

Long before Caleb successfully led the battle to the top of the mountain that he claimed for God, he was successful as a follower. Caleb was willing to follow orders in spying out the land; Caleb was willing to do things God's way even during the long travail of a forty-year journey through the wilderness; and Caleb, while never the primary leader, willingly submitted himself to the God-ordained spiritual influences in his life. Most believers will spend much, if not all of their lives and ministries, in a position where being able and willing to follow is of the utmost importance.

Illustration (faithful obedience)

Private Raymond Cote was in Germany with the 12th Infantry after World War II. During maneuvers, he was put on sentry duty to guard some pontoons on the banks of the Rhine. Because of an oversight, he was not relieved for six days. He knew the general order that states: "To quit my post only when properly relieved." So he stayed on duty day and night even when it rained heavily. Sympathetic farmers gave him food and milk. When he finally was relieved and got back to his outfit, his commanding officer praised his "strong sense of duty." But some of his buddies wisecracked that Cote had "a hole in his head." (Source unknown)

Illustration (obedience)

Roger Staubach, who led the Dallas Cowboys to victory in Super Bowl VI (1972), admitted that his position as a quarterback who didn't call his own signals was a source of trial for him. Coach Tom Landry sent in every play. He told Staubach when to pass and when to run; only in emergency situations could he change the play (and he had better be right!). Even though Staubach considered Coach Landry to have a "genius mind" when it came to football strategy, pride said that he should be able to run his own team. Staubach later said, "I faced up to the issue of obedience. Once I learned to obey, there was harmony, fulfillment, and victory." (contributed by James Dunn, www.sermoncentral.com)

B. AS A LEADER

Caleb knew the heart of God and tried to lead the people to do what God would have them to do. God had promised the people that they could win the victory in the land, and so Caleb's response to those who were fearful was, "Let us go up at once, and possess it; for we are well able to overcome it" (Numbers 13:30). God's Word guides people today who will take the lead in getting others to follow God's commands.

Illustration

He was a cobbler, a man who most would say was not well-equipped to do anything spectacular or even special. And yet God used William Carey to translate the Scriptures into forty-two languages, as well as to be instrumental in the founding of twenty churches. What was the secret to this man's success? It could be encapsulated in his timeless statement: "Attempt great things for God. Expect great things from God."

II. Remained Faithful

It is relatively easy to be faithful for a period of time while things are going smoothly, but God is looking for people who will remain faithful through the difficult times and through the valleys in life. Hebrews 11 lists many who remained faithful under very adverse circumstances.

A. ATTITUDE

NUMBERS 14:24

24 But **my servant Caleb**, because he had another spirit with him, and hath followed me fully, him will I bring into the land whereinto he went; and his seed shall possess it.

God's Word makes it clear that Caleb's spirit was very unlike that of the Israelites as a whole. A perusal of the narrative of their time in the wilderness shows that the spirit of the Israelites was very often one of complaining, murmuring, and discontent. Caleb, however, knew that God would fulfill His Word and give them the land that had been promised to them.

Illustration

"Attitude, not aptitude, determines altitude."—Dr. Curtis Hutson

Illustration (servant of Christ)

A nineteenth century painting shows a long row of beggars waiting in a soup line. They are all ragged and sleazy looking. But around the head of one, barely perceptible, is a halo. One of them is Christ! You may see no halo around the heads of your brothers and sisters in need, yet to serve them is to serve Christ, for the King is hidden in them. (Fredericksburg Bible Illustrator Supplements)

B. Obedience

Numbers 14:24

*24   But my servant Caleb, because he had another spirit with him, and **hath followed me fully**, him will I bring into the land whereinto he went; and his seed shall possess it.*

Obedience is a necessary part of everyone's life. We obey the rules at work if we want to keep our jobs. We obey the traffic laws for our own safety as well as for the safety of others. The question is, "To what degree are we obedient?" God's Word makes it very clear that Caleb was totally obedient. The Bible says that he followed Him fully, and in Numbers 32:12, it says he "wholly followed the Lord." One of the greatest challenges of a believer's life is to obey completely and immediately. Time after time throughout the Scriptures, we see people like Caleb who did obey when they were given a task, and God blessed and used them because of it.

Illustration

He was a pastor, a husband, and a father. As a faithful pastor in Bedford, England, John Bunyan was told that he must obtain a license from the crown in order to be permitted to proclaim God's Word. Knowing that this royal license could result in royal control over his preaching, he refused to accept such a license. He was imprisoned in the Bedford jail. His own daughter was sent to him, asking him to accept the license so he could come home. Yet, he remained faithful, and God used him to bless and challenge, not only his generation, but also millions of others with his allegorical novel *Pilgrim's Progress.*

III.   Remembered the <u>Promises</u>

God has many promises for His children. Unfortunately as believers, we often tend to forget the promises of God. We forget the fact that God will always keep His promises. In 2 Corinthians 1:20 the Bible says, "For all the promises of God in him are yea, and in him Amen...." This verse clearly teaches that you can trust the promises of God. God gave Caleb several promises, and he knew they were trustworthy.

A. THE PROMISE OF THE LAND

JOSHUA 14:12

12 *Now therefore give me this mountain,* **whereof the LORD spake in that day;** *for thou heardest in that day how the Anakims were there, and that the cities were great and fenced: if so be the LORD will be with me, then I shall be able to drive them out, as the LORD said.*

Only two of the adults who entered the wilderness would actually go into the land of Canaan. Those two were Caleb and Joshua. The Lord had said that He would drive out the inhabitants of the land, and they knew beyond a doubt that they could believe God. Their trust in their Lord would be rewarded with the ultimate victory.

The Apostle Paul was another man who knew that God could be trusted. Facing a terrible storm at sea and certain shipwreck, he declared this to the rest of his shipmates:

ACTS 27:25

25 *Wherefore, sirs, be of good cheer: for I believe God, that it shall be even as it was told me.*

B. THE PROMISE OF THE VICTORY

JOSHUA 14:12

12 *Now therefore give me this mountain,* **whereof the LORD spake in that day;** *for thou heardest in that day how the Anakims were there, and that the cities were great and fenced: if so be the LORD will be with me,* **then I shall be able to drive them out, as the LORD said.**

Although the enemy was mighty and the cities were large, Caleb knew that he could have victory. He knew this because he claimed the promise of God, who had told him that he

Lesson Two—Caleb—Mountain Claiming

would be able to drive them out. God has promised us victory in our lives, but unfortunately believers sometimes forget that "greater is he that is in you, than he that is in the world" (1 John 4:4). The New Testament further illustrates this when it says in 1 Corinthians 15:57, "…thanks be to God, which giveth us the victory through our Lord Jesus Christ." It is because of this promise that we can be steadfast and unmovable. God promises to give us the victory. There is no doubt that the writer of the song "Victory in Jesus" understood this well. Caleb claimed this victory at an advanced age (eighty-five!), and was obviously a blessing to his children and his children's children as well.

C. THE PROMISE OF THE AGE

JOSHUA 14:9–12

9 *And Moses sware on that day, saying, Surely the land whereon thy feet have trodden shall be thine inheritance, and thy children's for ever, because thou hast wholly followed the* LORD *my God.*

10 *And now, behold, the* LORD *hath kept me alive, as he said, these forty and five years, even since the* LORD *spake this word unto Moses, while the children of Israel wandered in the wilderness: and now, lo, I am this day fourscore and five years old.*

11 *As yet I am as strong this day as I was in the day that Moses sent me: as my strength was then, even so is my strength now, for war, both to go out, and to come in.*

12 *Now therefore give me this mountain, whereof the* LORD *spake in that day; for thou heardest in that day how the Anakims were there, and that the cities were great and fenced: if so be the* LORD *will be with me, then I shall be able to drive them out, as the* LORD *said.*

One of the encouraging things about the life of Caleb is that God used him even though he was past the age of eighty. It was a beautiful illustration that "If God be for us, who can be against us?" (Romans 8:31). Caleb won the victories and

29

claimed promises as a very advanced senior citizen. You are never too old to serve God!

Illustration

(Booker T. Washington describes meeting an ex-slave from Virginia in his book *Up from Slavery*): "I found that this man had made a contract with his master, two or three years previous to the Emancipation Proclamation, to the effect that the slave was to be permitted to buy himself, by paying so much per year for his body; and while he was paying for himself, he was to be permitted to labour where and for whom he pleased.

"Finding that he could secure better wages in Ohio, he went there. When freedom came, he was still in debt to his master some three hundred dollars. Not withstanding that the Emancipation Proclamation freed him from any obligation to his master, this black man walked the greater portion of the distance back to where his old master lived in Virginia, and placed the last dollar, with interest, in his hands.

"In talking to me about this, the man told me that he knew that he did not have to pay his debt, but that he had given his word to his master, and his word he had never broken. He felt that he could not enjoy his freedom till he had fulfilled his promise."

This man could not rest until he had kept his promise. We can be assured God takes His promises even more seriously.

Illustration (the promises of God must be claimed)

J. Wilbur Chapman related this in "Present-Day Parables": "When General Booth was in this country he told the story of a man who was starving to death, and the man received a check from a friend, promising to pay a certain amount of money to him. He held it up and danced around the room in his glee. His wife looks at him and says: 'Poor man, I was afraid it would be too much for him. He has suffered until he is unsettled mentally.' 'Wife,' he said, 'I am going to have it framed and hang it up. I will have it set to music and we will sing it every day.' And General Booth said he could have it framed, and could have it set to music and sing it every day of his life, sing it hour after hour until he died, and it would not do him any good if he did not take the check and demand payment. It is thus we treat God's promises. They are valueless without we present them to Him and believe them."

Conclusion

When a person is not purposefully engaging himself in a way that necessitates his reliance on God, he will default to a state of apathy. Caleb was careful at every stage of life to place his reliance firmly on God. This habit of trust enabled Caleb to remain faithful to the God on whom he so fervently relied. God blessed this confidence and made several promises to Caleb that he never forgot. Even when he reached what we would call old age—although Caleb didn't feel a bit old!—he remained faithful to the Lord and claimed the promises of God. We need more people like this today!

Study Questions

1. How old was Caleb when he said, "Give me this mountain"? How long had he waited to claim God's promise?
   Caleb was 85 years old and had waited for 45 years.

2. What is to be the GPS of the Christian's life?
   The Christian is to be guided by the Word of God.

3. How did the Lord Jesus Christ counter the temptations of Satan?
   He quoted the Word of God.

4. What Bible chapter is especially filled with examples of people who had faith and were faithful to God in challenging circumstances?
   Hebrews chapter 11

5. Realizing that the Bible states that Caleb "wholly followed the LORD," how would you rate yourself on following the Lord (on a scale of one to ten)?
   Answers will vary.

6. What promises of God are especially meaningful to you?
   Answers will vary.

7. Where do you especially need victory in your life right now?
   Answers will vary.

8. What promises of God would apply to this area where you need victory?
   Answers will vary.

Lesson Two—Caleb—Mountain Claiming

Memory Verse

Now therefore give me this mountain, whereof the LORD spake in that day; for thou heardest in that day how the Anakims were there, and that the cities were great and fenced: if so be the LORD will be with me, then I shall be able to drive them out, as the LORD said.
—JOSHUA 14:12

LESSON THREE

BARNABAS
The Encourager

Text

ACTS 11:22–26

22 *Then tidings of these things came unto the ears of the church which was in Jerusalem: and they sent forth Barnabas, that he should go as far as Antioch.*

23 *Who, when he came, and had seen the grace of God, was glad, and exhorted them all, that with purpose of heart they would cleave unto the Lord.*

24 *For he was a good man, and full of the Holy Ghost and of faith: and much people was added unto the Lord.*

25 *Then departed Barnabas to Tarsus, for to seek Saul:*

26 *And when he had found him, he brought him unto Antioch. And it came to pass, that a whole year they assembled themselves with the church, and taught much people. And the disciples were called Christians first in Antioch.*

Overview

Barnabas was a man who worked mainly behind the scenes. He was a generous man in the cause of the Lord, not only in the matter of his finances but also in his personal influence. He was one who took the time and effort to encourage people, and in fact the very name Barnabas means "the son of consolation." In particular, God used him to rescue and restore his nephew John Mark, who had been dismissed from Paul's missionary team.

Lesson Theme

All of us need encouragement from time to time, and we all remember times when a little encouragement made a great

35

difference to us. Perhaps we can also recall times when we were used by God to encourage someone else, and what a blessing that was to us as well. Through the scriptural narrative of several incidents in the life of Barnabas, we will see how we can be encouragers whom God can use to be great positive influences on the lives of others.

Lesson Goals

At the conclusion of the lesson, each student should:

1. Summarize the various incidents in the life of Barnabas that showed him to be an encourager
2. Summarize the results in the lives of those whom Barnabas encouraged
3. Consider and carry out specific ways of being an encouragement to others

Teaching Outline

Introduction

I. Gave to God
   A. Finance
   B. Influence

II. Served the Saints
   A. Exhorted the saints
   B. Encouraged his brother

III. Rescued the Rebuked
   A. Rescued John Mark
   B. Restored John Mark

Conclusion

LESSON THREE

BARNABAS
The Encourager

Text

ACTS 11:22–26

22 Then tidings of these things came unto the ears of the church which was in Jerusalem: and they sent forth Barnabas, that he should go as far as Antioch.

23 Who, when he came, and had seen the grace of God, was glad, and exhorted them all, that with purpose of heart they would cleave unto the Lord.

24 For he was a good man, and full of the Holy Ghost and of faith: and much people was added unto the Lord.

25 Then departed Barnabas to Tarsus, for to seek Saul:

26 And when he had found him, he brought him unto Antioch. And it came to pass, that a whole year they assembled themselves with the church, and taught much people. And the disciples were called Christians first in Antioch.

Introduction

Barnabas is an excellent illustration of someone we should all seek to imitate. While sometimes we look at the Apostle Paul and think

37

I can't do that or we look at Moses and may be intimidated by a man who was a leader to millions, Barnabas is someone who can be an example for each and every one of us. Barnabas was an encourager, the "son of consolation," and one who made a difference in the lives of many others.

I.   Gave to God

One of the most well-known verses in all of Scripture is John 3:16, which says, *"For God so loved the world that He gave...."* God gave His Son; the Son gave His life. Believers who truly desire to follow Jesus also will be involved in giving—and giving sacrificially. The life of Barnabas is a wonderful example of someone who was willing to give to God. He was generous both with his finances and with his personal influence.

A. FINANCE

ACTS 4:36–37

36   And Joses, who by the apostles was surnamed Barnabas, (which is, being interpreted, The son of consolation,) a Levite, and of the country of Cyprus,

37   Having land, sold it, and brought the money, and laid it at the apostles' feet.

God's Word states "where your treasure is, there will your heart be also" (Matthew 6:21). Barnabas gave to the cause of Christ by selling his land. It has been well said, regarding earthly treasures, that we cannot take them with us—but we can send them on ahead. Those who trust God in the area of giving will find that they cannot outgive God.

LUKE 6:38

38   Give, and it shall be given unto you; good measure, pressed down, and shaken together, and running over, shall men give into your bosom. For with the same measure that ye mete withal it shall be measured to you again.

Lesson Three—Barnabas—The Encourager

MALACHI 3:10–11

10 *Bring ye all the tithes into the storehouse, that there may be meat in mine house, and prove me now herewith, saith the LORD of hosts, if I will not open you the windows of heaven, and pour you out a blessing, that there shall not be room enough to receive it.*

11 *And I will rebuke the devourer for your sakes, and he shall not destroy the fruits of your ground; neither shall your vine cast her fruit before the time in the field, saith the LORD of hosts.*

B. INFLUENCE

ACTS 9:27

27 *But Barnabas took him, and brought him to the apostles, and declared unto them how he had seen the Lord in the way, and that he had spoken to him, and how he had preached boldly at Damascus in the name of Jesus.*

Our influence—for good or for bad—can have a very powerful effect in the lives of others. When Saul of Tarsus, who had been making havock—rampaging, ravaging, and devastating the church—claimed a sudden conversion and acceptance of Jesus Christ as Lord, people were undoubtedly skeptical of his statement and afraid of him. Barnabas, however, realized that his conversion was real, and used his influence to bring him into the fellowship of the church. The generosity of Barnabas in putting his own reputation on the line for the sake of a new believer undoubtedly made a great difference in the life of Paul, and therefore to all who have since been influenced by Paul. The Apostle Paul spoke of the ongoing power of influence to the young pastor Timothy.

2 TIMOTHY 2:2

2 *And the things that thou hast heard of me among many witnesses, the same commit thou to faithful men, who shall be able to teach others also.*

39

Illustration

R.G. LeTourneau was a mechanical genius who accepted the Lord Jesus Christ as his Saviour. As his business grew, he continued to give a greater and greater percentage of his income to the work of the Lord. With each ensuing gift, it seemed as though there were multiplied blessings. Soon, LeTourneau's earthmoving equipment was being sold around the world, and he became a multi-millionaire. LeTourneau used these monies to support missionaries and churches, and he even built a Christian college. During the last major portion of his life, R.G. LeTourneau was giving over 90% of his income to the cause of Christ. He had learned that it's good to give to God.

Illustration (biblical living)

C.S. Lewis put it well when he said, "I'm afraid biblical charity is more than merely giving away that which we could afford to do without anyway."

Illustration (giving—quote)

John Bunyan, author of *The Pilgrim's Progress* wrote, "A man there was, and they called him mad; the more he gave, the more he had."

Illustration (giving)

Marquis de Lafayette was a French general and politician who joined the American Revolution and became a friend of George Washington. An influential man in the U.S. and France, Lafayette was also a man of compassion. The harvest of 1782 was a poor one, but the manager of his estate had filled his barns with wheat. "The bad harvest has raised the price of wheat," said his manager. "This is the time to sell."

Lafayette thought about the hungry peasants in the villages and replied, "No, this is the time to give."

Real love is often measured by our willingness to let go of what we possess. (Fredericksburg Bible Illustrator Supplements)

Illustration (giving)

A farmer was known for his generous giving, but his friends could not understand how he could give so much away and yet remain so prosperous. One day a spokesman for his friends said, "We can't understand you. You give far more than the rest of us and yet you always seem to have more to give." "Oh, that is easy to explain," the farmer said. "I keep shoveling into God's bin and God keeps shoveling into mine, but God has the bigger shovel!" Here was a man whose ethics of giving were controlled by the power of an indwelling Lord. (Fredericksburg Bible Illustrator Supplements)

II. Served the Saints

Once people decide to give to God, they will also seek to serve. The same attitude that leads a believer to be generous with his money and his influence will lead him also to give generously of his time and his abilities. Here again, those who serve will find themselves in imitation of Christ. "O To Be Like Thee, Blessed Redeemer" runs the old hymn—is that the desire of your heart? Then be willing to give, and be willing to serve—and go beyond just being willing: live out that willingness on a daily basis. As you faithfully do this, to quote another hymn, you will be "More Like the Master."

Matthew 20:26–28

26 But it shall not be so among you: but whosoever will be great among you, let him be your minister;

27 And whosoever will be chief among you, let him be your servant:

28 Even as the Son of man came not to be ministered unto, but to minister, and to give his life a ransom for many.

In many ways, Barnabas illustrated Christ-likeness in his life. He realized that the ministry was not all about him, but about being a blessing to those around him.

Illustration (job vs. ministry)

Do you have a job in this church…or do you have a ministry? There is a difference!

- If you are doing it because no one else will, it's a job. If you're doing it to serve the Lord, it's a ministry.
- If you're doing it just well enough to get by, it's a job. If you're doing it to the best of your ability, it's a ministry.
- If you'll do it only so long as it doesn't interfere with other activities, it's a job. If you're committed to staying with it even when it means letting go of other things, it's a ministry.
- If you quit because no one praised you or thanked you, it was a job. If you stay with it even though no one seems to notice, it's a ministry.
- If you do it because someone else said that it needs to be done, it's a job. If you are doing it because you are convinced it needs to be done, it's a ministry.
- It's hard to get excited about a job. It's almost impossible not to get excited about a ministry.
- If your concern is success, it's a job. If your concern is faithfulness, it's a ministry.
- People may say "well done" when you do your job. The Lord will say "well done" when you complete your ministry.
- An average church is filled with people doing jobs. A great church is filled with people who are performing a ministry. (www.sermonillustrations.com)

A. EXHORTED THE SAINTS

ACTS 11:23

*23 Who, when he came, and had seen the grace of God, was glad, **and exhorted them all**, that with purpose of heart they would cleave unto the Lord.*

Lesson Three—Barnabas—The Encourager

The biblical word *cleave* here means "to bond in a very personal way" (as a husband would cleave to his wife, Genesis 2:24). Barnabas urged the Christians to bond with the Lord. Think of a strong glue that you might use around your home or shop to "bond" things together. What an amazing challenge for believers today—that our words and lives would encourage other people to literally become one with the Lord Jesus Christ. Barnabas wanted the believers to cleave to the Lord in a very personal and possessive way.

B. ENCOURAGED HIS BROTHER

There is no question that the body of Christ as a whole needs encouragement. Proverbs 16:21 says that "the sweetness of the lips increaseth learning." Truth taught in an encouraging manner will be effective. Barnabas demonstrated this Old Testament truth in his New Testament life, as he deliberately went looking for Saul and brought him into the fellowship of the believers at Antioch. Is it possible that the Christ-likeness of this man Barnabas—a man who would seek someone who was considered an enemy, for the purpose of bringing him back for a wonderful reconciliation and great usefulness—is what prompted others to bestow the term "Christian" on those believers?

ACTS 11:25–26

25 Then departed Barnabas to Tarsus, for to seek Saul:

26 And when he had found him, he brought him unto Antioch. And it came to pass, that a whole year they assembled themselves with the church, and taught much people. And the disciples were called Christians first in Antioch.

LUKE 19:10

10 For the Son of man is come to seek and to save that which was lost.

1. He loved the unlovely.

There would have been very few who would have met Saul of Tarsus without struggling with feelings of reproach and

43

Lessons from Legends

disdain; yet, Barnabas knew that Saul was a new creature in Christ. Often times, church families seem to take a "wait and see" attitude with new believers. This is wrong. The Bible teaches us that they are now new creatures in Christ and should be treated in a way that reflects this reality.

2. He loved the Gentiles.

Acts 15:12

12   Then all the multitude kept silence, and gave audience to Barnabas and Paul, declaring what miracles and wonders God had wrought among the Gentiles by them.

Barnabas did not only love the Jews who came to Christ: he also loved the Gentiles. He realized that Christ loved the Gentile as He did the Jew. Paul and Barnabas began to minister to the Gentiles and share what Christ had done with a group of people who were looked upon with haughty disdain by the mainstream Jewish populace. Before you arrogantly condemn these Jews as foolish and prideful, ask yourself, "What groups are looked down upon today by the church, that the Lord would have us reach out to?" Maybe it is the homeless bum, the unwed mother, the drug addict, the AIDS-infected young person, or the alcoholic. There is no doubt that God loves these people just as much as He loves you. Barnabas realized this and would certainly have reached out to them as well.

Illustration (Amy Carmichael)

A beautiful illustration of someone who loved the unlovely can be found in Amy Carmichael. Amy was born in 1867, and, after hearing Hudson Taylor speak, felt God calling her to a mission field. Miss Carmichael spent fifty-five years in India without ever taking a single furlough. She founded an orphanage and a mission in Dohnabur. She was in the ministry of reaching that group of people whom Jesus called the "least of these." This giving woman began her ministry by developing a Sunday school class for girls who she called "shawlies." These were young ladies who could not afford to own even a hat! Several people wrote her while she was in India and asked what missionary life was like. She lovingly answered, "Missionary life is simply a chance to die." After giving her life to reaching as many of the unlovely as she could, Amy Carmichael declared, "One can give without loving, but one cannot love without giving."

III.   Rescued the Rebuked (John Mark)

Illustration (refusing to give up on someone; taken from Daily Bread, 5/1/99)

You may recall the news story in the New York Times several years ago about a high altitude crisis of British Airways Flight 5390. The pilot of the passenger plane was sucked out of the cabin window onto the nose cone of the jet after its windshield blew out at 23,000 feet. What took place next is incredible.

Timothy Lancaster, the pilot, had just pointed to his house in Abingdon, when a loud explosion blew out the windshield. Pressurized air bursting from inside the plane pulled him partway out. Outside, the 320 mph airstream bent the upper half of his body against the jet's fuselage.

Several of the aircraft's 81 passengers said they watched in horror as crew members frantically wrestled to pull the pilot back in the cockpit. At one point, the crew was faced with a terrible possibility: would they have to push their captain out to free the controls? The co-pilot shook his head and shouted to the others, "Hold on if you possibly can." However, they were able to readjust the body enough to fly the plane. The jet went into a dive. With half of Mr. Lancaster's body hanging outside, the co-pilot flew the aircraft towards Southampton Airport (70 miles southwest of London).

Crew members, who clung to his ankles for 15 minutes, were encouraged by the co-pilot who kept yelling, "Hold on with all your might—we're almost there!" He finally landed the plane safely in southern England. Mr. Lancaster was taken to the hospital suffering from shock, a fractured elbow and wrist, and frostbite on one hand.

More than likely, you will never experience anything as dramatic and dangerous as this rescue. Yet, lives and souls are in jeopardy all around us. A friend's marriage is exploding. A brother is being "sucked" back into his old ways. A sister, who has messed up many times, creates the question, "Do we continue to help or should we just cut our losses and move on?" Unfortunately, we experience many losses due to decisions and circumstances. However, in many cases what we need to do is continue to be prayerfully persistent and encouraging. Refuse to give up on them and "hold on if you possibly can!"

A. Rescued John Mark
Acts 15:36–39

36 And some days after Paul said unto Barnabas, Let us go again and visit our brethren in every city where we have preached the word of the Lord, and see how they do.

37 And Barnabas determined to take with them John, whose surname was Mark.

38 But Paul thought not good to take him with them, who departed from them from Pamphylia, and went not with them to the work.

39 And the contention was so sharp between them, that they departed asunder one from the other: and so Barnabas took Mark, and sailed unto Cyprus;

When John Mark was evicted from the missionary team, Barnabas took him in. It is the forsaken, chastised, or disciplined believers who often need just a little urging to come back in the right direction. Those left to themselves often turn their backs on that which is right and go on their own way. John Mark had been expelled, but Barnabas decided that he was worth rescuing. There is no doubt that if we in the church would take the time to observe those around us,

46

we, too, could see people who could be rescued with some timely effort.

B. Restored John Mark

2 Timothy 4:11

11   *Only Luke is with me. Take Mark, and bring him with thee: for he is profitable to me for the ministry.*

The best part of the story of Barnabas is, as Paul Harvey would have said, "the rest of the story." As Paul neared the end of his ministry, he requested Timothy to bring Mark with him and gave one of the greatest compliments of Scripture, "…for he is profitable to me for the ministry."

There is no doubt that if believers would pattern their lives after the life of Barnabas, that many could be restored to the ministry again today. It is necessary to note that long before Barnabas ever went on a missionary journey, the church had extended to him the right hand of fellowship (Galatians 2:9). There is no doubt that this acceptance had an unforgettable impact on the life of Barnabas, and compelled him to manifest that acceptance to others. Truly, here is a man who made a difference!

Conclusion

Few men have had a testimony as great as Joses (Barnabas). In fact, his testimony was so strong that those around him decided to change his name so that it would reflect his true personality. His very identity was changed because of his attitude. Barnabas was a man who happily and willingly gave to God, served other Christians, and sought to aid those who had fallen away from their former dedication to the faith of Christ. He was a great encouragement. If you were renamed to reflect your attitude, what would your name be?

Lessons from Legends

Study Questions

1. What does the name "Barnabas" mean?
    The name Barnabas means "the son of consolation."

2. List two areas in the life of Barnabas where he showed a willingness to give.
    He gave of his finances and he gave of his influence.

3. What former persecutor of Christians did Barnabas bring into the fellowship of the church?
    Barnabas brought the new convert Paul into the fellowship of the church.

4. To which outcast group of people did Barnabas minister?
    Barnabas (and Paul) ministered to the Gentiles.

5. What disgraced and rejected Christian brother did Barnabas restore to fellowship and usefulness?
    Barnabas restored his nephew John Mark, whom Paul had expelled from the missionary team.

6. List some specific ways in which you can act as a servant.
    Answers will vary.

7. List some specific ways in which you can be an encouragement to others.
    Answers will vary, but may include: having a positive attitude, speaking kindly to everyone, and paying special attention to someone who may be discouraged.

Lesson Three—Barnabas—The Encourager

8.   Specifically, what will you do to try to encourage someone this week?
     Answers will vary.

Memory Verses

*Who, when he came, and had seen the grace of God, was glad, and exhorted them all, that with purpose of heart they would cleave unto the Lord. For he was a good man, and full of the Holy Ghost and of faith: and much people was added unto the Lord.—*ACTS 11:23–24

LESSON FOUR

JOHN
The Beloved

Text

JOHN 13:21–25

21 When Jesus had thus said, he was troubled in spirit, and testified, and said, Verily, verily, I say unto you, that one of you shall betray me.

22 Then the disciples looked one on another, doubting of whom he spake.

23 Now there was leaning on Jesus' bosom one of his disciples, whom Jesus loved.

24 Simon Peter therefore beckoned to him, that he should ask who it should be of whom he spake.

25 He then lying on Jesus' breast saith unto him, Lord, who is it?

Overview

Of all the twelve disciples, Jesus had a special love for John. Wherever his Lord was, John tried to be as close as possible. After the ascension of Christ, John exhibited courage as one of the "pillars" of the early church. He was faithful to the Lord and was honored with the special vision of the Revelation of Jesus Christ.

Lesson Theme

While we know that the Lord Jesus Christ loves all of His children, there are qualities we can acquire and things we can do to draw even closer to Him. We can gain these qualities by learning from and emulating the life of John, the beloved disciple.

Lesson Goals

At the conclusion of the lesson, each student should:

1. Understand how John earned the title of "the beloved disciple" during the earthly ministry of Christ
2. Understand how John showed faithfulness for so many decades after Christ went back to Heaven
3. Decide to live close to the Lord on a daily basis

Teaching Outline

Introduction

I. Beloved of Christ
   A. Close in communion
   B. Close in court
   C. Close at the Crucifixion

II. Brave in Character
   A. Stood against heresy
   B. Stood against backsliding

III. Blessed in Comparison
   A. Faithful in trials
   B. Faithful over time

Conclusion

LESSON FOUR

JOHN
The Beloved

Text

JOHN 13:21–25

21 When Jesus had thus said, he was troubled in spirit, and testified, and said, Verily, verily, I say unto you, that one of you shall betray me.
22 Then the disciples looked one on another, doubting of whom he spake.
23 Now there was leaning on Jesus' bosom one of his disciples, whom Jesus loved.
24 Simon Peter therefore beckoned to him, that he should ask who it should be of whom he spake.
25 He then lying on Jesus' breast saith unto him, Lord, who is it?

Introduction

It is an amazing thing to think that a man could be called "the beloved" of the Lord. To be beloved by the Lord Jesus Christ is truly a special honor. The Lord Jesus Christ had twelve men whom He took to mentor and train for three years. Of these twelve men,

53

there were three who would be considered the "inner circle": Peter, James, and John. Of these three, it was John who was chosen as the "beloved." In one of the most famous pictures ever painted of the Lord Jesus Christ, Leonardo da Vinci's *The Last Supper*, John is portrayed laying his head on the Lord Jesus Christ. John made a conscious decision to stay close to his Master. He was not the first to do this.

I. <u>Beloved</u> of Christ

Illustration (staying close to God's man)

Because Elisha was determined to stick close to his mentor Elijah, he was awarded a double portion of his spirit:

> *And it came to pass, when the LORD would take up Elijah into heaven by a whirlwind, that Elijah went with Elisha from Gilgal. And Elijah said unto Elisha, Tarry here, I pray thee; for the LORD hath sent me to Bethel. And Elisha said unto him, **As the LORD liveth, and as thy soul liveth, I will not leave thee.** So they went down to Bethel. And the sons of the prophets that were at Bethel came forth to Elisha, and said unto him, Knowest thou that the LORD will take away thy master from thy head to day? And he said, Yea, I know it; hold ye your peace. And Elijah said unto him, Elisha, tarry here, I pray thee; for the LORD hath sent me to Jericho. And he said, **As the LORD liveth, and as thy soul liveth, I will not leave thee.** So they came to Jericho. And the sons of the prophets that were at Jericho came to Elisha, and said unto him, Knowest thou that the LORD will take away thy master from thy head to day? And he answered, Yea, I know it; hold ye your peace. And Elijah said unto him, Tarry, I pray thee, here; for the LORD hath sent me to Jordan. And he said, **As the LORD liveth, and as thy soul liveth, I will not leave thee.** And they two went on. And fifty men of the sons of the prophets went, and stood to view afar off: and they two stood by Jordan. And Elijah took his mantle, and wrapped it together, and smote the waters, and they were divided hither and thither, so that they two went over on dry ground. **And it came to pass, when they were gone over, that Elijah said unto Elisha, Ask what I shall do***

Lesson Four—John—The Beloved

for thee, before I be taken away from thee. And Elisha said, I pray thee, let a double portion of thy spirit be upon me. And he said, Thou hast asked a hard thing: nevertheless, if thou see me when I am taken from thee, it shall be so unto thee; but if not, it shall not be so. And it came to pass, as they still went on, and talked, that, behold, there appeared a chariot of fire, and horses of fire, and parted them both asunder; and Elijah went up by a whirlwind into heaven. And Elisha saw it, and he cried, My father, my father, the chariot of Israel, and the horsemen thereof. And he saw him no more: and he took hold of his own clothes, and rent them in two pieces. He took up also the mantle of Elijah that fell from him, and went back, and stood by the bank of Jordan; And he took the mantle of Elijah that fell from him, and smote the waters, and said, Where is the LORD God of Elijah? and when he also had smitten the waters, they parted hither and thither: and Elisha went over.—2 KINGS 2:1–14

Illustration (quote by A. W. Tozer—communion)

"God has not bowed to our nervous haste nor embraced our machine age. The man who would know God must give time to Him."

Illustration (hymn, "Take Time to Be Holy")

Take time to be holy,
Speak oft with thy Lord;
Abide in Him always
And feed on His word.
Make friends of God's children,
Help those who are weak
Forgetting in nothing
His blessing to seek.

Take time to be holy,
The world rushes on;
Spend much time in secret
With Jesus alone.
By looking to Jesus,
Like Him thou shalt be—

Thy friends in thy conduct
His likeness will see.

Take time to be holy,
Let Him be thy guide,
And run not before Him,
Whatever betide.
In joy or in sorrow
Still follow thy Lord,
And, looking to Jesus,
Still trust in His word.

Take time to be holy,
Be calm in thy soul—
Each thought and each motive
Beneath His control.
Thus led by His Spirit
To fountains of love,
Thou soon shalt be fitted
For service above.
(words by William D. Longstaff; music by George C. Stebbins)

A. CLOSE IN COMMUNION

JOHN 13:23–26

*23 **Now there was leaning on Jesus' bosom one of his disciples, whom Jesus loved.***

24 Simon Peter therefore beckoned to him, that he should ask who it should be of whom he spake.

25 He then lying on Jesus' breast saith unto him, Lord, who is it?

26 Jesus answered, He it is, to whom I shall give a sop, when I have dipped it. And when he had dipped the sop, he gave it to Judas Iscariot, the son of Simon.

There are numerous incidents in the New Testament when John was in close communion with the Lord. We have already mentioned his being close to the Lord at the Last Supper. He was close to the Lord at the time of the Transfiguration. He was close to the Lord when Jesus went

Lesson Four—John—The Beloved

alone to pray. He was close to the Lord when the Lord went down into the ship. John made it a personal habit to stay as close as he possibly could to the Lord.

Illustration (quote by Brennan Manning)

"When we draw near enough to hear Jesus' heartbeat, we discover, as John did, that we are His beloved."

B. CLOSE IN COURT

JOHN 18:15–16

15 And Simon Peter followed Jesus, **and so did another disciple**: that disciple was known unto the high priest, and went in with Jesus into the palace of the high priest.

16 But Peter stood at the door without. Then went out that other disciple, which was known unto the high priest, and spake unto her that kept the door, and brought in Peter.

The Bible makes it very clear that John was closest to the Lord in the difficult times (John always spoke of himself modestly). As for ourselves, we often find that it is easier to get excited about church and the things of the Lord when the economy is good, the family is doing well, and when everyone is happy. While Jesus was on trial at the court, only two of his followers were there: Peter and John. This is a great challenge for Christians to stick with other believers in difficult times.

B. CLOSE AT THE CRUCIFIXION

JOHN 19:26–27

26 When Jesus therefore saw his mother, **and the disciple standing by, whom he loved**, he saith unto his mother, Woman, behold thy son!

27 Then saith he to the disciple, Behold thy mother! And from that hour that disciple took her unto his own home.

It has been said that people remember how you start and how you finish. At the time of the crucifixion of the Lord Jesus

57

Christ, John the Beloved was there. Jesus had a special love for John, trusted him greatly because of his faithfulness, and chose him to care for His mother Mary after His decease. And so John did, taking Mary into his own home as though she were his own mother, for the rest of her life. This is a challenge to us to be "finishers" in our Christian lives.

II. <u>Brave</u> in Character

Although it may seem obvious, we need to realize that standing for right involves standing against things that are wrong. The eighteenth century political thinker Edmund Burke has a famous quote attributed to him: "All that is necessary for evil to prosper is for good men to do nothing." John loved Christ, and this love constrained him to stand against those who stood against the Lord. Later, while instructing young Christians in the truth, John told believers that those who did not confess the name of the Lord Jesus Christ were not true Christians at all, but rather deceivers (2 John 7).

Illustration (courage, from a speech by Senator John McCain)

"As you may know, I spent five and one half years as a prisoner of war during the Vietnam War. In the early years of our imprisonment, the NVA kept us in solitary confinement; or two or three to a cell. In 1971 the NVA moved us from these conditions of isolation into large rooms with as many as 30 to 40 men to a room. This was, as you can imagine, a wonderful change and was a direct result of the efforts of millions of Americans on behalf of a few hundred POWs 10,000 miles from home.

"One of the men who moved into my room was a young man named Mike Christian. Mike came from a small town near Selma, Alabama. He didn't wear a pair of shoes until he was 13 years old. At 17, he enlisted in the US Navy. He later earned a commission by going to Officer Training School. He then became a Naval Flight Officer and was shot down and captured in 1967. Mike had

Lesson Four—John—The Beloved

a keen and deep appreciation of the opportunities this country, and our military, provide for people who want to work and want to succeed. As part of the change in treatment, the Vietnamese allowed some prisoners to receive packages from home. In some of these packages were handkerchiefs, scarves and other items of clothing. Mike got himself a bamboo needle.

"Over a period of a couple of months, he created an American flag and sewed it on the inside of his shirt. Every afternoon, before we had a bowl of soup, we would hang Mike's shirt on the wall of the cell and say the Pledge of Allegiance. I know the Pledge of Allegiance may not seem the most important part of our day now, but I can assure you that in that stark cell, it was indeed the most important and meaningful event.

"One day the Vietnamese searched our cell, as they did periodically, and discovered Mike's shirt with the flag sewn inside, and removed it. That evening they returned, opened the door of the cell, and for the benefit of all of us, beat Mike Christian severely for the next couple of hours. Then, they opened the door of the cell and threw him in. We cleaned him up as well as we could. The cell in which we lived had a concrete slab in the middle on which we slept. Four naked light bulbs hung in each corner of the room.

"After the excitement died down, I looked in the corner of the room, and sitting there beneath that dim light with a piece of red cloth, another shirt and his bamboo needle, was my friend, Mike Christian. He was sitting there with his eyes almost shut from the beating he had received, making another American flag."

A. STOOD AGAINST HERESY

2 JOHN 7

7   *For many deceivers are entered into the world, who confess not that Jesus Christ is come in the flesh. This is a deceiver and an antichrist.*

John was not the least bit hesitant when it came to pointing out and standing against false doctrine. Many today would call him "intolerant." The terms "deceiver" and "antichrist" are not used by those who want to get along with

59

everybody. John cared most about getting along with his precious Lord, and he stood squarely and emphatically against those who stood against Christ and the truths of His Word.

B. Stood against backsliding

2 John 8

8 *Look to yourselves, that we lose not those things which we have wrought, but that we receive a full reward.*

John knew that there was but one way to get to Heaven, and that was through his Lord and Saviour. It is in the Gospel of John that we find that well-known verse, "Jesus saith unto him, I am the way, the truth, and the life: no man cometh unto the Father, but by me" (John 14:6). In the current religious climate, ecumenicalism—religious unity with no regard for absolute truth, the philosophy that "many roads lead to God"—is widely accepted and even encouraged. Like John, we as Christians need to stand for the Lord Jesus Christ as the Way, the Truth, and the Life, instead of backsliding down the slippery slope of compromise. John challenged the believers not to lose the things that they had gained. He reminded them of the reward that awaited those who would stand faithfully for the truth.

III. Blessed in Comparison

Because he was beloved of Jesus Christ, John experienced some unique blessings. John was blessed in that he was able to see things happen that other disciples not as close were not able to see (the Transfiguration is one example). John was blessed in that he was able to see things that no other living human being had ever seen (to him was given the astounding visions of the Revelation). God also blessed him with longevity of life and an extended time of ministry. We believe that John was the only one who was not martyred for his faith, yet we know that he was faithful until the Lord called him home.

Lesson Four—John—The Beloved

Illustration (faithful in trials and over time)

On Queen Elizabeth's "official birthday" some years back, she conferred honors on a number of her subjects. One person honored was a sixty-year-old postman in northern Wales, a fellow with the unroyal name of Jones. Because Jones, who came from a family delivering Welsh mail for 150 years, had "not missed a day's service in 43 years and got the mail through despite snow, storms and floods," the Queen bestowed the British Empire Medal upon him, expressing the gratitude of the nation.

If an earthly majesty would bestow such a superlative honor on a man for faithfulness in so simple a task as delivering the mail, do you not think the Majesty of Heaven will be even more diligent to make certain each of His subjects receives a proper and gracious award for faithful service? Of course He will! This review will be according to quality, not necessarily quantity; it will not be how much, but what kind. (Dr. Robert Sumner, source "The Biblical Evangelist," date of issue unknown)

A. Faithful in <u>trials</u>

REVELATION 1:9

9 *I John, who also am your brother, and companion in tribulation, and in the kingdom and patience of Jesus Christ, was in the isle that is called Patmos, for the word of God, and for the testimony of Jesus Christ.*

John spent the latter years of his life in exile on the isle of Patmos. While some would find this a place of discouragement, which might lead to despondency and maybe a critical, negative spirit, John talked about being on the island for the purpose of the Word of God and for the testimony of Jesus Christ. John rejoiced in that, as he had rejoiced many years before when he was among those counted worthy to suffer shame for the name of Christ (Acts 5:41). What a challenge for each of us to maintain a good testimony and a godly outlook if we find ourselves in unpleasant circumstances! It has been rightfully said that trials reveal what we truly are. Can you rejoice as you suffer for the Lord?

61

B. Faithful over time

One reason John was blessed more than the others was because he was faithful over time. Easton's Bible Dictionary says that John lived until about A.D. 98. The Bible relates several stories of those who, at the end of their lives, made decisions that were not Christ-like or God-honoring. Noah had great faith, yet shame ensued soon after the ark landed (Genesis 9:20–23). Lot, who started off as a companion of righteous and faithful Abraham, ended up with disgrace in a cave (Genesis 19:30–38). Samson began his life with such promise, but ended his life blinded and grinding like an animal for the Philistines (Judges 16:21). Speaking of regrets, the poet Whittier put it this way: "For of all sad words of tongue or pen, the saddest are these: 'It might have been!'" With John the Beloved, it can be said he lived his life fully and wholly for his Lord, right to the end.

Conclusion

The apostle John had a very unique relationship with the Saviour. He was "the beloved disciple." This special place did not just randomly fall to John. He was a very brave and dedicated Christian, and this dedication was blessed by God. How are you doing? Are you brave in your character? Are you a disciple of Christ whom He can trust to obey and follow Him? Will you stick close to Him at all times, as John did?

Lesson Four—John—The Beloved

Study Questions

1. What special blessing did Elisha receive as a reward for staying close to his mentor Elijah?
   Elisha received a double portion of the spirit and power of Elijah.

2. List instances in the Gospels where it was apparent that John had an especially close relationship with Christ.
   John was one of the three witnesses of the Transfiguration. John leaned on Jesus' breast at the Last Supper. John was with Jesus in the Garden when He went alone to pray. John was one of the two disciples who followed Jesus to His trial. John was close to Jesus while He was hanging on the Cross, and the Lord entrusted John with the future care of Mary.

3. What motivated John to stand against those who stood against the Lord?
   The love of Christ constrained him.

4. List some specific challenges that John gave the believers in his second epistle.
   Answers may vary, but should include: Stand for the truth; do not lose or let go of the things you have learned, stood for, and gained. Do not compromise; do not backslide.

5. In what ways was John's life (after Christ went back to Heaven) different from the other disciples?
   John had a long, extended ministry; he lived to be an old man; we believe he was the only disciple not to die a martyr for the faith.

Lessons from Legends

6.   Where did John spend the later years of his life, and why was he there?
John spent his later years in exile on the isle of Patmos because he had stood for the Word of God and the testimony of Jesus Christ.

7.   What special incident happened to John in that place?
Jesus Christ appeared to him personally and gave him the Revelation.

8.   In what specific ways can we imitate the life of John and understand more of what it means to be beloved of the Lord?
Answers will vary, but may include: make a conscious decision to stay close to the Lord, stay close to the Lord in difficult times, stay close to the Lord for the long-term, stand against false doctrine and backsliding

Memory Verse

And thou shalt love the Lord thy God with all thy heart, and with all thy soul, and with all thy mind, and with all thy strength: this is the first commandment.—MARK 12:30

LESSON FIVE

JEREMIAH
Heart of Compassion

Text

JEREMIAH 4:14–19

14 *O Jerusalem, wash thine heart from wickedness, that thou mayest be saved. How long shall thy vain thoughts lodge within thee?*

15 *For a voice declareth from Dan, and publisheth affliction from mount Ephraim.*

16 *Make ye mention to the nations; behold, publish against Jerusalem, that watchers come from a far country, and give out their voice against the cities of Judah.*

17 *As keepers of a field, are they against her round about; because she hath been rebellious against me, saith the LORD.*

18 *Thy way and thy doings have procured these things unto thee; this is thy wickedness, because it is bitter, because it reacheth unto thine heart.*

19 *My bowels, my bowels! I am pained at my very heart; my heart maketh a noise in me; I cannot hold my peace, because thou hast heard, O my soul, the sound of the trumpet, the alarm of war.*

Overview

The Old Testament prophet Jeremiah cared so deeply for his people and was so pained by their wickedness that he has become known as the "Weeping Prophet." He had a fervent love for the lost and, although at one point in his life he almost quit the ministry, he could not keep himself from proclaiming the Word of God. He remained loyal to his Lord, faithfully preaching the message of God and His righteousness in spite of persecutions. He was able to do this because of his reliance on God's mercy and faithfulness.

65

Lesson Theme

Caring comes with a cost. In Jeremiah we see a faithful man of God who was willing to bear the burden of caring for a people who for the most part did not care. His example should inspire and instruct us in being the type of Christians God wants us to be and the type of Christians this world needs to see: a people who truly care in our hearts and in our actions.

Lesson Goals

At the conclusion of the lesson, each student should:

1. Understand how Jeremiah's burden for his people affected the way he ministered to them
2. Understand how Jeremiah showed loyalty to the Lord
3. Decide to be a caring, compassionate Christian

Teaching Outline

Introduction

    I. Love for the Lost
       A. Affected heart
       B. Affected actions

   II. Loyal to the Lord
       A. In his declarations
       B. In his tribulations

  III. Light of His Life
       A. Mercy
       B. Faithfulness

Conclusion

LESSON FIVE

JEREMIAH
Heart of Compassion

Text

JEREMIAH 4:14–19

14 O Jerusalem, wash thine heart from wickedness, that thou mayest be saved. How long shall thy vain thoughts lodge within thee?

15 For a voice declareth from Dan, and publisheth affliction from mount Ephraim.

16 Make ye mention to the nations; behold, publish against Jerusalem, that watchers come from a far country, and give out their voice against the cities of Judah.

17 As keepers of a field, are they against her round about; because she hath been rebellious against me, saith the LORD.

18 Thy way and thy doings have procured these things unto thee; this is thy wickedness, because it is bitter, because it reacheth unto thine heart.

19 My bowels, my bowels! I am pained at my very heart; my heart maketh a noise in me; I cannot hold my peace, because thou hast heard, O my soul, the sound of the trumpet, the alarm of war.

Introduction

At one point in David's life, he felt that absolutely no one cared what he was going through.

PSALM 142:4

4   I looked on my right hand, and behold, but there was no man that would know me: refuge failed me; no man cared for my soul.

Maybe there has been a time in your life when you have felt the same way, and you remember how precious it was to you when someone reached out with a helping hand from a compassionate heart. People who truly care can truly make a difference. Let's look into the life of Jeremiah and learn from a man who was not afraid or ashamed to care about others.

I.   Love for the Lost

Of all the prophets of God, there is no doubt that Jeremiah was one who had a great compassion for his people. The man, known as the "Weeping Prophet," was greatly affected by the backsliding and sin that surrounded him. Unlike many, he did not allow himself to become calloused: he cared enough to cry, and he cared enough to do something to resolve the needs with which he was faced.

Illustration (J. Hudson Taylor, on the parable of the ninety-nine sheep)

"Can all the Christians of England," he wrote, "sit still with folded arms while these multitudes [in China] are perishing—perishing for lack of knowledge—for lack of that knowledge which England possesses so richly, which has made England what England is and made us what we are? What does the Master teach us? Is it not that if one sheep out of a hundred be lost, we are to leave the ninety and nine and seek that one? But here the proportions are almost reversed, and we stay at home with the one sheep, and take no heed to the ninety and nine perishing ones!"

Taylor became convinced that a special organization was needed for the evangelization of inland China—to go beyond the five treaty ports to which nearly all missionary work had been confined. He was determined not to cut the financial ground from under the feet of the older missionary societies, but what form should such an organization take?

He began making plans for recruiting twenty-four missionaries: two for each of eleven inland provinces of China that were without a missionary, and two for Mongolia. It was a visionary plan that would have left experienced missionaries breathless: at the time, a host of seasoned missionary organizations had, all told, only some ninety Protestant missionaries in China. Taylor single-handedly wanted to increase that by over 25 percent.

This would be an enormous financial commitment, so Taylor opened a bank account under the name of the China Inland Mission (CIM). Soon he had money and five missionary volunteers to send to China—even before he had formally committed himself to head a new missions society. (Author: Roger Steer, Online Christian History #52)

A. Affected HEART

JEREMIAH 4:18–19

18   Thy way and thy doings have procured these things unto thee; this is thy wickedness, because it is bitter, because it reacheth unto thine heart.

*19   **My bowels, my bowels! I am pained at my very heart; my heart maketh a noise in me;** I cannot hold my peace, because thou hast heard, O my soul, the sound of the trumpet, the alarm of war.*

God's Word teaches us that our eyes affect our hearts. What we see and consider affects how we feel. It was so with the Lord Jesus Christ.

MATTHEW 9:36

36   But when he [Christ] saw the multitudes, he was moved with compassion on them, because they fainted, and were scattered abroad, as sheep having no shepherd.

MATTHEW 6:22–23

22 *The light of the body is the eye: if therefore thine eye be single, thy whole body shall be full of light.*

23 *But if thine eye be evil, thy whole body shall be full of darkness. If therefore the light that is in thee be darkness, how great is that darkness!*

Jeremiah states here that his heart was pained and that he was literally hearing the cry of his heart regarding the Jewish people. When God speaks to our hearts, we too need to respond. But not only must we be straining to hear, we must be sensitive to respond. Jeremiah felt actual physical pain because his heart was hurting so badly. When was the last time your heart was broken so badly over someone's sin that you even shed a tear?

B. AFFECTED ACTIONS

JEREMIAH 20:9

9 *Then I said, I will not make mention of him, nor speak any more in his name. But his word was in mine heart as a burning fire shut up in my bones, and I was weary with forbearing, and I could not stay.*

Because God spoke to the heart of Jeremiah, he had to respond. It was God's Word that inspired him and forced him to action. Jeremiah was so overcome with the message of the Word of God that he literally could not withhold himself from delivering it even though, out of discouragement, he had vowed to leave the ministry. Peter and John told the hostile authorities, "For we cannot but speak the things which we have seen and heard" (Acts 4:20). Paul told the Corinthians, "…necessity is laid upon me; yea, woe is unto me, if I preach not the gospel!" (1 Corinthians 9:16). We, too, need to let God's Word work in us and through us. If God's Word permeates our lives as it should, there will be an inevitable overflow that will affect all those around us.

II. Loyalty to the Lord

Despite the fact that it was neither a popular position nor the position of the majority, Jeremiah realized the importance of being loyal to the Lord.

A. IN HIS DECLARATIONS

JEREMIAH 42:4

*4 Then Jeremiah the prophet said unto them, I have heard you; behold, I will pray unto the LORD your God according to your words; **and it shall come to pass, that whatsoever thing the LORD shall answer you, I will declare it unto you; I will keep nothing back from you.***

Jeremiah made it clear that he desired to speak only that which the Lord told him to speak. The prophet Micaiah said something very similar: "As the LORD liveth, what the LORD saith unto me, that will I speak" (1 Kings 22:14). Whether it is a parent with a child, a pastor with a church, or any other relationship, it is important that what is declared as truth are the words and the precepts of God and not merely personal opinions.

ACTS 20:27

27 For I have not shunned to declare unto you all the counsel of God.

1 CORINTHIANS 2:12–13

12 Now we have received, not the spirit of the world, but the spirit which is of God; that we might know the things that are freely given to us of God.

13 Which things also we speak, not in the words which man's wisdom teacheth, but which the Holy Ghost teacheth; comparing spiritual things with spiritual.

REVELATION 22:18–19

18 For I testify unto every man that heareth the words of the prophecy of this book, If any man shall add unto these things, God shall add unto him the plagues that are written in this book:

19   And if any man shall take away from the words of the book of this prophecy, God shall take away his part out of the book of life, and out of the holy city, and from the things which are written in this book.

B. IN HIS TRIBULATIONS

JEREMIAH 38:6

6   Then took they Jeremiah, and cast him into the dungeon of Malchiah the son of Hammelech, that was in the court of the prison: and they let down Jeremiah with cords. And in the dungeon there was no water, but mire: so Jeremiah sunk in the mire.

Jeremiah was faithful to the Lord even when imprisoned and sinking in the mire of the dungeon. He understood what the hymn writer Thomas Chisholm meant when he penned "Great is Thy Faithfulness": "All I have needed Thy hand hath provided. Great is Thy faithfulness, Lord, unto me." Jeremiah is a beautiful illustration of one who found out that Christ's strength is sufficient in a miserable situation.

Illustration (Loyalty to Christ, Charles Swindoll)

"To Renounce Your Commitment to Christ, Leave Now!"

Stories from the underground church in Russia never fail to jolt us awake. I came across another one just this past week. A house church in a city of the Soviet Union received one copy of the Gospel by Luke, the only Scripture most of these Christians had ever seen. They tore it into small sections and distributed them among the body of believers. Their plan was to memorize the portion they had been given, then on the next Lord's Day they would meet and redistribute the scriptural sections.

On Sunday these believers arrived inconspicuously in small groups throughout the day so as not to arouse the suspicion of KGB informers. By dusk they were all safely inside, windows closed and doors locked. They began by singing a hymn quietly but with deep emotion. Suddenly, the door was pushed open and in walked two soldiers with loaded automatic weapons at the ready. One shouted, "All right—everybody line up against the wall. If you wish to renounce your commitment to Jesus Christ, leave now!"

Two or three quickly left, then another. After a few more seconds, two more.

"This is your last chance. Either turn against your faith in Christ," he ordered, "or stay and suffer the consequences."

Another left. Finally, two more in embarrassed silence with their faces covered, slipped out into the night. No one else moved. Parents with small children trembling beside them looked down reassuringly. They fully expected to be gunned down or at best, to be imprisoned.

After a few minutes of complete silence, the other soldier closed the door, looked back at those who stood against the wall and said, "Keep your hands up—but this time in praise to our Lord Jesus Christ, brothers and sisters. We, too, are Christians. We were sent to another house church several weeks ago to arrest a group of believers." The other soldier interrupted, "But, instead, we were converted! We have learned by experience, however, that unless people are willing to die for their faith, they cannot be fully trusted."

III.   Light of His Life

Throughout the Bible, we can see themes evident in the lives of many great men of God. For John the Baptist, the theme seems to be the coming Messiah; for the Apostle Paul, it appears as the Gospel of the risen Saviour; for Jeremiah, his constant theme is the mercy and faithfulness of God.

A.   MERCY

LAMENTATIONS 3:21–22

21   *This I recall to my mind, therefore have I hope.*

22 It is of the LORD's mercies that we are not consumed, because his compassions fail not.

Jeremiah talked about the mercies of God, but he did more than simply talk about God's mercies: he himself was merciful to the people of Israel. While it would have been easy to give up on them because of their sin and wrongdoing, he prayed, he wept, and he encouraged his countrymen to come back to God.

B. FAITHFULNESS

LAMENTATIONS 3:23

*23 They are new every morning: **great is thy faithfulness.***

Thomas Paine wrote during the American Revolution about the "summer soldiers" and "sunshine patriots" who would draw back from serving their country in its time of crisis. This was not the case with Jeremiah. He was faithful in times of hardship, deprivation, and imprisonment. He was dependent upon God's faithfulness, and he ever modeled faithfulness in his own life.

Illustration (God's mercy, John Newton)

A portion of Newton's last will and testament read, "I commit my soul to my gracious God and Saviour, who mercifully spared and preserved me, when I was an apostate, a blasphemer, and an infidel, and delivered me from that state…into which my obstinate wickedness had plunged me; and Who has been pleased to admit me, though most unworthy, to preach His glorious gospel. I rely with humble confidence upon the atonement, and mediation of the Lord Jesus Christ, God and Man, which I have often proposed to others, as the only foundation whereupon a sinner can build his hope, trusting that He will guard and guide me through the uncertain remainder of my life, and that He will then admit me into His presence in His heavenly kingdom."

On his tombstone are these words: "John Newton, Clerk, once an infidel and libertine, a servant of slaves in Africa, was, by the rich mercy of our Lord and Saviour Jesus Christ, preserved, restored, pardoned, and appointed to preach the faith he had long labored to destroy" (John Revell, *Baptist Press*).

Conclusion

Jeremiah was a phenomenal example of a man whose heartbeat was in rhythm with the heart of the Lord. God spoke to Jeremiah, and he received the Word of God with personal passion and fervor. Deep in the heart of Jeremiah, God instilled a great love for the lost souls of Israel. This heart-breaking love, combined with a steadfast loyalty to the Lord, caused Jeremiah's life to be a light that shone into the darkness of the wicked world around him. I challenge you to search your own heart. Do you have a compassion for the lost? Do you have a burning desire to live your life in such a way that the glory of your God is clearly shown to those around you? If not, my friend, you may want to search your heart in the presence of God until you discover and correct the problem.

Study Questions

1. Why has Jeremiah become known as the "Weeping Prophet"?
   Jeremiah has become known as the "Weeping Prophet" because of his great compassion and tears for the people of God, and for his pain over their sin.

2. God's Word teaches us that our eyes affect our hearts. What is meant by this?
   Answers may vary, but the concept is that what we see and meditate upon determines our feelings and emotions. As Jeremiah saw the sinfulness and spiritual needs of his people, his compassion grew.

3. Why did Jeremiah say that he could not keep from preaching the Word of God?
   He said that the Word was in his heart like a burning fire shut up in his bones.

4. Describe one specific trial Jeremiah suffered because of his faithful stand for the Word of God.
   He was put in a dungeon, where he sank in the mire.

5. What was the constant theme of Jeremiah's preaching?
   Jeremiah constantly emphasized the mercy and faithfulness of God.

6. How can we become more compassionate toward other people?
   Answers will vary, but could include the following: stop thinking about ourselves so much and begin to think about others, get involved in ministries, draw closer to the Lord and begin to see people as He sees them.

Lesson Five—Jeremiah—Heart of Compassion

7. Are you living in such a way that the Lord would consider you a loyal Christian? In what areas do you need to become more loyal?
    Answers will vary.

8. In what ways can you demonstrate mercy in your daily life?
    Answers will vary.

Memory Verse

Oh that my head were waters, and mine eyes a fountain of tears, that I might weep day and night for the slain of the daughter of my people!—JEREMIAH 9:1

LESSON SIX

RUTH
From Defeat to Victory

Text

RUTH 1:19–22

19 So they two went until they came to Bethlehem. And it came to pass, when they were come to Bethlehem, that all the city was moved about them, and they said, Is this Naomi?

20 And she said unto them, Call me not Naomi, call me Mara: for the Almighty hath dealt very bitterly with me.

21 I went out full, and the LORD hath brought me home again empty: why then call ye me Naomi, seeing the LORD hath testified against me, and the Almighty hath afflicted me?

22 So Naomi returned, and Ruth the Moabitess, her daughter in law, with her, which returned out of the country of Moab: and they came to Bethlehem in the beginning of barley harvest.

Overview

Ruth knew both depths of sorrow and heights of blessing. From those depths, she followed her mother-in-law Naomi back to the land of the people of God. There she worked hard and faithfully, and God rewarded her with favor in the sight of Naomi's kinsman Boaz. They married, and Boaz and Ruth ultimately became the great-grandparents of King David and earthly ancestors of the Lord Jesus Christ.

Lesson Theme

Every one of us will face times of failure, defeat, temptations, and despair. It is important for us to realize that God never forsakes His children, and no matter what the situation, there is always

79

hope in the Lord. We need to follow godly direction and be faithful. In His own time, God will bring us to blessing and victory.

Lesson Goals

At the conclusion of the lesson, each student should:

1. Understand the importance of following those who are following God
2. Realize that a whole-hearted attitude is necessary to successful labor for the Lord
3. Decide to be a follower and a worker whom God can bless

Teaching Outline

Introduction

   I. Faithful in Following
      A. Followed Naomi's path
      B. Followed Naomi's counsel
        1. Go to Boaz's field.
        2. Go to Boaz's feet.

  II. Fervent in Laboring
      A. Went to the harvest
      B. Stayed in the harvest

 III. Favored with Blessing
      A. Immediate needs met
      B. Permanent needs met

Conclusion

LESSON SIX

RUTH
From Defeat to Victory

Text

RUTH 1:19–22

19 So they two went until they came to Bethlehem. And it came to pass, when they were come to Bethlehem, that all the city was moved about them, and they said, Is this Naomi?

20 And she said unto them, Call me not Naomi, call me Mara: for the Almighty hath dealt very bitterly with me.

21 I went out full, and the LORD hath brought me home again empty: why then call ye me Naomi, seeing the LORD hath testified against me, and the Almighty hath afflicted me?

22 So Naomi returned, and Ruth the Moabitess, her daughter in law, with her, which returned out of the country of Moab: and they came to Bethlehem in the beginning of barley harvest.

Introduction

Often when people are defeated, they think their lives are over and that God cannot use them. But God's Word often shows that a defeat is merely the closing of a chapter, and that God is about to

81

open up a new opportunity and a new chance to serve Him. As we will see today, such was the case with Ruth.

I. <u>Faithful</u> in Following

God is looking for one primary qualification in a follower: it is not intelligence or ability; it is *faithfulness*. It is not education or a record of past achievements; it is *faithfulness*. No matter what other attributes or gifts one may have, a lack of faithfulness will make the Christian useless in God's work.

1 CORINTHIANS 4:2
2   *Moreover it is required in stewards, that a man be found faithful.*

MATTHEW 16:24
24   *Then said Jesus unto his disciples, If any man will come after me, let him deny himself, and take up his cross, and follow me.*

JOHN 10:27
27   *My sheep hear my voice, and I know them, and they follow me:*

JOHN 12:26
26   *If any man serve me, let him follow me; and where I am, there shall also my servant be: if any man serve me, him will my Father honour.*

Illustration

In "Everyday Discipleship for Ordinary People," Stuart Briscoe wrote about a fellow minister who was asked to officiate at a funeral for a war veteran. Briscoe recalls, "The dead man's military friends wished to have a part in the service at the funeral home, so they requested the pastor to lead them down to the casket, stand with them for a solemn moment of remembrance, and then lead them out through the side door. This he proceeded to do, but...picked the wrong door. The result was that they marched with military precision into a broom closet, in full view of the mourners...." Briscoe suggests at least two principles that can be gained from that story: "First, if you're going to lead, make sure you know where you're going. Second, if you're going to follow, make sure that you are following someone who knows what he is doing!" (Author Unknown, Provided by Student Discipleship Ministries, TX)

A. FOLLOWED NAOMI'S PATH

RUTH 1:22

22 *So Naomi returned, and Ruth the Moabitess,* **her daughter in law, with her,** *which returned out of the country of Moab: and they came to Bethlehem in the beginning of barley harvest.*

In Genesis 24:27 the servant of Abraham, who was sent to find a bride for Isaac, rejoiced to say, "I being in the way, the LORD led me." As we are faithful to follow, God leads us further. One of the ways that God leads is through His people—and not just through professional Christian leaders or experienced counselors. You may not consider yourself a leader, but you can rest assured that someone is looking to you for an example. No matter who you are, God wants to use you to show someone else the right way to go. In Ruth 1:22, we see that Naomi decided to return to the city of Bethlehem and Ruth decided to follow her. This was a step of faith on Ruth's part, but, as God's Word clearly states, "whatsoever is not of faith is sin" (Romans 14:23). That is the choice we face in every decision: faith or sin. Ruth was about to embark on a path of miraculous providence and blessing, and it all began with her willingness to follow. It should be noted that following always involves leaving. In following Naomi, Ruth left her friends, her family, and the place of her birth, but God had so much more for her in a new place.

B. FOLLOWED NAOMI'S COUNSEL

A wise person, contrary to what one may think, is not someone who knows it all. Wise people are willing to listen and learn. Wise people understand their need for more wisdom!

Lessons from Legends

PROVERBS 1:5

5 *A wise man will hear, and will increase learning; and a man of understanding shall attain unto wise counsels:*

Ruth had told Naomi when they left Moab, "...whither thou goest, I will go; and where thou lodgest, I will lodge: thy people shall be my people, and thy God my God" (Ruth 1:16). When they reached Bethlehem, Naomi told Ruth both where to go and what to do. Ruth trusted Naomi and did what she was told. Naomi knew that there was a place where Ruth could access the blessings of her family heritage and guided Ruth to it.

1. Go to Boaz's field.

RUTH 2:1–2

1 *And Naomi had a kinsman of her husband's, a mighty man of wealth, of the family of Elimelech; and his name was Boaz.*

2 *And Ruth the Moabitess said unto Naomi, Let me now go to the field, and glean ears of corn after him in whose sight I shall find grace.* **And she said unto her, Go, my daughter.**

2. Go to Boaz's feet.

RUTH 3:6–7

6 *And she went down unto the floor, and did according to all that her mother in law bade her.*

7 *And when Boaz had eaten and drunk, and his heart was merry, he went to lie down at the end of the heap of corn:* **and she came softly, and uncovered his feet, and laid her down.**

Naomi not only told Ruth where to go, but she told her whom to go to. She knew that the answer for Ruth was to get to the right person—that being Boaz, for he was the one who could meet her needs.

We, too, need to get to the one who can meet our needs, the Lord Jesus Christ. God's Word commands us

Lesson Six—Ruth—From Defeat to Victory

to "come boldly unto the throne of grace" (Hebrews 4:16). It is not enough to believe that help is available: we must actively go to Him. Not only that, but we need to direct others to the same Lord Who can and will meet their needs as well.

JOHN 1:41

41 He first findeth his own brother Simon, and saith unto him, We have found the Messias, which is, being interpreted, the Christ.

JOHN 1:45

45 Philip findeth Nathanael, and saith unto him, We have found him, of whom Moses in the law, and the prophets, did write, Jesus of Nazareth, the son of Joseph.

JOHN 4:29

29 Come, see a man, which told me all things that ever I did: is not this the Christ?

II. <u>Fervent</u> in Laboring

Pastor Paul Chappell has often said, "Laziness is the scourge of the ministry." While it is true that people have different levels of gifts and responsibilities, no one has more and no one has less than twenty-four hours in the day. Each of us is held accountable for what we do with those hours. We are to "redeem (make wise and sacred use of) the time, because the days are evil" (Ephesians 5:16). God's Word challenges us, "Whatsoever thy hand findeth to do, do it with thy might" (Ecclesiastes 9:10). We can easily see that Ruth believed this.

Illustration

Ten Best Excuses when you are caught napping...

10. "They told me at the blood bank this might happen."
9. "This is just a 15 minute power-nap like they raved about in that time management course you sent me to."

85

Lessons from Legends

8. "Whew! Guess I left the top off the Wite-Out. You probably got here just in time!"

7. "I wasn't sleeping! I was meditating on the mission statement and envisioning a new paradigm."

6. "I was testing my keyboard for drool resistance."

5. "I was doing a highly specific Yoga exercise to relieve work-related stress. Are you discriminatory toward people who practice Yoga?"

4. "Why did you interrupt me? I had almost figured out a solution to our biggest problem."

3. "The coffee machine is broken...."

2. "Someone must've put decaf in the wrong pot...."

And the #1 best thing to say if you get caught sleeping at your desk...

1. "...in Jesus' name. Amen."

Illustration (List of work rules issued by proprietor Zachary U. Geiger in 1872):

1. Daily sweep the floors.
2. Wash the windows once a week.
3. Bring in a bucket of water and a scuttle of coal.
4. Make pens carefully.
5. Hours are 7 AM to 8 PM. Closed on Sabbath. Each employee is expected to spend the SABBATH by attending CHURCH and contributing liberally to the cause of the LORD.
6. Men will be given an evening off each week for courting purposes, or two evenings a week if they go regularly to CHURCH.
7. After an employee has spent 13 hours of labor in the office, he should spend the time reading the BIBLE and other good books while contemplating the glories and building up of the KINGDOM.
8. Every employee should lay aside from each pay a goodly sum of his earnings for his benefit during his declining years, so that he will not become a burden upon the charity of his betters.

9. Any employee who smokes Spanish cigars, uses liquor in any form, gets shaved at a barber shop, or frequents pool and public halls, will give me good reason to suspect his WORTH, INTENTIONS, and HONESTY.

10. The employee who has performed his labours faithfully and without fault for a period of five years in my service and who has been THRIFTY and attentive to his RELIGIOUS DUTIES, is looked upon by his fellowmen as a SUBSTANTIAL and law abiding CITIZEN, will be given an increase of five cents per day in his pay, providing a just return in profits from the business permits it.

Be worthy of your hire.

A. WENT TO THE HARVEST

RUTH 2:3

3 And she went, and came, and gleaned in the field after the reapers: and her hap was to light on a part of the field belonging unto Boaz, who was of the kindred of Elimelech.

Ruth went to where the harvest was taking place. She knew that there was reaping going on, and she wanted to be a part of it. It is very common for people who are serious about reaping to spend time with others who are also serious about reaping. Farmers gravitate to other farmers. People who enjoy gardening love to talk with others who share their interest. Such was the case with Ruth.

B. STAYED IN THE HARVEST

RUTH 2:23

23 So she kept fast by the maidens of Boaz to glean unto the end of barley harvest and of wheat harvest; and dwelt with her mother in law.

It has been well said that people remember how you start and how you finish. We find here that Ruth stayed in the field until the end of the harvest. She did not gather a little bit and say, "That is enough for today," but she stuck with the job until the harvesting was done. For believers today, the harvest time will not end until the Lord Jesus chooses either to call us home via death or via the sound of the trumpet. God's Word clearly states this, and we are told to occupy until He comes.

LUKE 19:13

13 And he called his ten servants, and delivered them ten pounds, and said unto them, Occupy till I come.

Illustration: The Ant and the Grasshopper (revised)

ORIGINAL VERSION: The ant works hard in the withering heat all summer long, building his house and laying up supplies for the winter. The grasshopper thinks he's a fool and laughs and dances and plays the summer away. Come winter, the ant is warm and well fed. The grasshopper has no food or shelter so he dies out in the cold.

MODERN AMERICAN VERSION: The ant works hard in the withering heat all summer long, building his house and laying up supplies for the winter. The grasshopper thinks he's a fool and laughs and dances and plays the summer away. Come winter, the shivering grasshopper calls a press conference and demands to know why the ant should be allowed to be warm and well fed while others are cold and starving.

CBS, NBC, and ABC show up to provide pictures of the shivering grasshopper next to a video of the ant in his comfortable home with a table filled with food.

America is stunned by the sharp contrast. How can it be that, in a country of such wealth, this poor grasshopper is allowed to suffer so?

Then a representative of the NAGB (The National Association of Green Bugs) shows up on Nightline and charges the ant with green bias, and makes the case that the grasshopper is the victim of 30 million years of greenism.

Kermit the Frog appears on Oprah with the grasshopper, and everybody cries when he sings "It's not easy being green."

Bill and Hillary Clinton make a special guest appearance on the CBS Evening News to tell a concerned Dan Rather that they will do everything they can for the grasshopper who has been denied the prosperity he deserves by those who benefited unfairly during the Reagan summers.

Richard Gephardt exclaims in an interview with Peter Jennings that the ant has gotten rich off the back of the grasshopper, and calls for an immediate tax hike on the ant to make him pay his "fair share."

Finally, the EEOC drafts the "Economic Equity and Anti-Greenism Act" retroactive to the beginning of the summer. The ant is fined for failing to hire a proportionate number of green bugs and, having nothing left to pay his retroactive taxes, his home is confiscated by the government.

Hillary gets her old law firm to represent the grasshopper in a defamation suit against the ant, and the case is tried before a panel of federal hearing officers that Bill appointed from a list of single-parent welfare moms who can only hear cases on Thursday's between 1:30 and 3:00 PM.

The ant loses the case.

The story ends as we see the grasshopper finishing up the last bits of the ant's food, while the government house he's in, which just happens to be the ant's old house, crumbles around him since he doesn't know how to maintain it. The ant has disappeared in the snow. And on the TV, which the grasshopper bought by selling most of the ant's food, they are showing Bill Clinton standing before a wildly applauding group of Democrats and Republicans announcing that a new era of "fairness" has dawned in America.

III. <u>Favored</u> with Blessing

We as parents delight to meet the needs of our children and will do whatever is necessary to take care of them. God is a much more faithful and capable Father than any of us could be, and we can rest assured that He will take good care of His children as well. But going beyond just the basic needs, we need to desire God's blessing on our lives. We spoke earlier of faithfulness: it is the key to following God, and it is the key to the blessings of God.

PROVERBS 28:20

20   A faithful man shall abound with blessings...

Illustration

There are so many miraculous ways throughout the Bible where God met specific needs:

The famine in Israel—God used Joseph to preserve his family (Genesis 42–50).

The escape from Egypt—God's people crossed the Red Sea on dry ground (Exodus 14).

The wilderness wanderings—God provided manna every day (Exodus 16).

Crossing of the Jordan—Again, the Israelites crossed on dry ground (Joshua 3).

The times of the Judges—Again and again God provided His people with deliverers from oppression (Judges 2).

David—God gave him strength and courage to overcome the lion and the bear and the Philistine giant (1 Samuel 17).

Solomon—He desired wisdom above all; God gave him wisdom— and honor and riches and peace as well (1 Kings 3).

Elijah—God used ravens to feed him (1 Kings 17).

The widow woman—She honored God and God's man and saw God provide in a wonderful way (1 Kings 17).

Daniel, Shadrach, Meshach, and Abednego—They honored God and saw His miraculous protection (Daniel 3 and 6).

The poor in spirit, the mourners, the meek, those hungering and thirsting after righteousness, the needy of all descriptions—No one who ever came to Jesus with a sincere heart went away without the need being met abundantly (Matthew 5).

God clearly promises that if we will put Him first, He will see to it that we are well-cared for. He takes good care of the birds and

Lesson Six—Ruth—From Defeat to Victory

the flowers, and we have no need to doubt that He will take even better care of us—the crown of His creation.

MATTHEW 6:24–33

24 No man can serve two masters: for either he will hate the one, and love the other; or else he will hold to the one, and despise the other. Ye cannot serve God and mammon.

25 Therefore I say unto you, Take no thought for your life, what ye shall eat, or what ye shall drink; nor yet for your body, what ye shall put on. Is not the life more than meat, and the body than raiment?

26 Behold the fowls of the air: for they sow not, neither do they reap, nor gather into barns; yet your heavenly Father feedeth them. Are ye not much better than they?

27 Which of you by taking thought can add one cubit unto his stature?

28 And why take ye thought for raiment? Consider the lilies of the field, how they grow; they toil not, neither do they spin:

29 And yet I say unto you, That even Solomon in all his glory was not arrayed like one of these.

30 Wherefore, if God so clothe the grass of the field, which to day is, and to morrow is cast into the oven, shall he not much more clothe you, O ye of little faith?

31 Therefore take no thought, saying, What shall we eat? or, What shall we drink? or, Wherewithal shall we be clothed?

32 (For after all these things do the Gentiles seek:) for your heavenly Father knoweth that ye have need of all these things.

33 But seek ye first the kingdom of God, and his righteousness; and all these things shall be added unto you.

God's Word teaches us that every good and perfect gift comes from Him. He is the source of blessing.

JAMES 1:17

17 Every good gift and every perfect gift is from above, and cometh down from the Father of lights, with whom is no variableness, neither shadow of turning.

It is a beautiful thing to see how God met the needs of both Ruth and Naomi.

A. IMMEDIATE NEEDS MET

RUTH 2:15–16

15 *And when she was risen up to glean, Boaz commanded his young men, saying, Let her glean even among the sheaves, and reproach her not:*
16 *And let fall also some of the handfuls of purpose for her, and leave them, that she may glean them, and rebuke her not.*

Each and every day that Ruth went into the field, she was able to glean (in other words, to gather that which the reapers left behind) enough food for her daily needs. The Bible uses a beautiful phrase when it states that there were "handfuls of purpose" that were left for her. Although the field was not hers, she was being watched over and cared for. God's Word says that He will not see the righteous forsaken nor His seed begging bread.

PSALM 37:25

25 *I have been young, and now am old; yet have I not seen the righteous forsaken, nor his seed begging bread.*

B. PERMANENT NEEDS MET

RUTH 4:13

13 **So Boaz took Ruth, and she was his wife:** *and when he went in unto her, the LORD gave her conception, and she bare a son.*

Ultimately, Ruth became the bride of Boaz and a part of his family. God gave them a son who was to be a part of the lineage of the Lord Jesus Christ (Matthew 1:1–16, notice verse 5). It is an amazing thing to look at some of the women whom God used to maintain the royal line of David that would someday result in the birth of the Lord Jesus Christ. Whether it was Rahab, Bathsheba, Tamar, or Ruth, we are reminded that God is looking for people that He can use to further His cause.

Conclusion

Just as Esther was a wonderful example of love and grace, Ruth is an equally fantastic example of faithfulness and fervency. No matter what trials God brought into her life, no matter how many immense and sudden changes she had to endure, Ruth remained faithful to her authority and fervent in her labor and, for this, she was favored with blessing from her God. The God Ruth served is the same God we serve today. We should remain faithful no matter what He allows to enter our lives, and we should be fervent in our labor. How are you doing with your service to your God?

Study Questions

1. Where was Ruth's original home, and to where did she follow Naomi?

   Ruth was from the land of Moab, and when her husband died she followed her widowed mother-in-law back to Bethlehem.

2. What did Ruth say to Naomi to express her willingness to follow?

   Ruth 1:16–17—"And Ruth said, Intreat me not to leave thee, or to return from following after thee: for whither thou goest, I will go; and where thou lodgest, I will lodge: thy people shall be my people, and thy God my God: Where thou diest, will I die, and there will I be buried: the LORD do so to me, and more also, if ought but death part thee and me."

3. When Naomi and Ruth returned to Bethlehem, where did Naomi send Ruth?

   Naomi sent Ruth to the fields, to glean after the reapers.

4. Explain the term "handfuls of purpose."

   Boaz saw that Ruth was a hard worker, and prompted his men to leave a little extra grain in the field for her to gather.

5. What does God promise us if we will seek first His kingdom and His righteousness?

   He promises to meet all of our needs without our having to worry about them.

6. What can you do to be a better worker—in your family, at your job, in your church?

   Answers will vary.

Lesson Six—Ruth—From Defeat to Victory

7. What adversities are you facing today that tempt you to be discouraged?
Answers will vary.

8. What Bible verses show you the way to overcome these adversities and find the way to victory?
Answers will vary.

Memory Verses

And Ruth said, Intreat me not to leave thee, or to return from following after thee: for whither thou goest, I will go; and where thou lodgest, I will lodge: thy people shall be my people, and thy God my God: Where thou diest, will I die, and there will I be buried: the LORD do so to me, and more also, if ought but death part thee and me.—RUTH 1:16–17

LESSON SEVEN

JOB
Trusting in Tribulations

Text

JOB 23:8–12

8   Behold, I go forward, but he is not there; and backward, but I cannot perceive him:

9   On the left hand, where he doth work, but I cannot behold him: he hideth himself on the right hand, that I cannot see him:

10   But he knoweth the way that I take: when he hath tried me, I shall come forth as gold.

11   My foot hath held his steps, his way have I kept, and not declined.

12   Neither have I gone back from the commandment of his lips; I have esteemed the words of his mouth more than my necessary food.

Overview

By all earthly standards, Job was a good man. Even God pointed him out to Satan as someone special. In this lesson we will see why and how the severest of trials came to Job, and how after a period of suffering and questioning, Job was eventually exalted by God when he humbled himself.

Lesson Theme

All of us have wondered at times why we suffer and why others suffer. God has a purpose in permitting trials to come into our lives. If our lives were always smooth and everything were easy, we would never grow much in our faith. Learning to trust God through our trials leads to triumph.

97

Lesson Goals

At the conclusion of the lesson, each student should:

1. Understand why Job was chosen to undergo the trials that came to him
2. Understand how Job maintained his faith during these trials
3. Decide to triumph through trust rather than be defeated through discouragement

Teaching Outline

Introduction

I. Testimony
   A. Perfect and upright
   B. Feared God
   C. Eschewed evil

II. Trials
   A. Financial trials
   B. Family trials
   C. Physical trials

III. Triumph
   A. Enlightenment
   B. Enrichment

Conclusion

LESSON SEVEN

JOB
Trusting in Tribulations

Text

JOB 23:8–12

8   Behold, I go forward, but he is not there; and backward, but I cannot perceive him:

9   On the left hand, where he doth work, but I cannot behold him: he hideth himself on the right hand, that I cannot see him:

10   But he knoweth the way that I take: when he hath tried me, I shall come forth as gold.

11   My foot hath held his steps, his way have I kept, and not declined.

12   Neither have I gone back from the commandment of his lips; I have esteemed the words of his mouth more than my necessary food.

Introduction

The Word of God states that rain falls on both the just and the unjust (Matthew 5:45). In our heads we know this to be true and normal. In our hearts may be a different expectation. We tend to think that if we are doing what is right, everything will go right,

99

Lessons from Legends

or at least *should* go right. Although this thought is certainly appealing, it is not a Bible truth. Because of our false expectations, we sometimes question God unjustly. God does not promise things will always go well, but He does promise His unfailing grace through the trials. Alfred Edersheim wrote: "We cannot understand the meaning of many trials; God does not explain them. To explain a trial would be to destroy its object, which is that of calling forth simple faith and implicit obedience." In the annals of Scripture, there is no one who was more tested and tried than Job. J. Sitlow Baxter said, "The theme of [Job] is blessing through suffering." James 5:11 declares, "Ye have heard of the patience of Job...." Without a doubt, there is much we can learn from the life of this great man.

I. <u>Testimony</u>

One man said "One ought to live his life in such a way that the pastor can tell the truth at the funeral." Another said, "Live your life in such a way that your family would not be ashamed to sell your parrot to the town gossip." A.W. Tozer said that we may be known by the following: "1) What we want most. 2) What we think about most. 3) How we use our money. 4) What we do with our leisure time. 5) The company we enjoy. 6) Who and what we admire. 7) What we laugh at." In Job chapter 1, we see what God said about Job.

A. Perfect and upright

Job 1:1

1   There was a man in the land of Uz, whose name was Job; and that man was perfect and upright, and one that feared God, and eschewed evil.

According to Strong's Lexicon, "perfect" and "upright" are synonymous in this passage. Job was literally living a life that was based on upright decisions—decisions that were not

100

Lesson Seven—Job—Trusting in Tribulations

simply upright before the world, but were upright before God. Dr. Bob Jones, Sr., was famous for many pithy phrases, among them the simple and powerful instruction, "Do right!" Job was a man who did right. The most powerful thing about the recording of Job's life of righteousness was that this testimony was given him by God Himself.

B. FEARED GOD

JOB 1:1

*1   There was a man in the land of Uz, whose name was Job; and that man was perfect and upright, **and one that feared God**, and eschewed evil.*

Throughout the Scriptures, the concept of fearing God deals with respecting God and His position. Job certainly had a holy respect for God. He understood and clearly stated throughout this book that God was the creator of the universe, that He had all power and that God could be trusted. God wants His creation to fear Him and to respect Him for who He is and for what He can do. Job did this, and God was pleased.

C. ESCHEWED EVIL

JOB 1:1

*1   There was a man in the land of Uz, whose name was Job; and that man was perfect and upright, and one that feared God, **and eschewed evil**.*

Finally, the Lord tells us that Job was a man who hated evil. God's plan for the believer is to love righteousness and flee from evil. The world wants us to toy with evil and to laugh at evil, but God wants us to hate it.

PSALM 97:10

10   Ye that love the LORD, hate evil: he preserveth the souls of his saints; he delivereth them out of the hand of the wicked.

HEBREWS 1:9

9   Thou hast loved righteousness, and hated iniquity; therefore
God, even thy God, hath anointed thee with the oil of gladness
above thy fellows.

God tells us that although we are *in* the world, we are not
to be *of* the world.

1 JOHN 2:15–17

15   Love not the world, neither the things that are in the world.
If any man love the world, the love of the Father is not in him.
16   For all that is in the world, the lust of the flesh, and the lust
of the eyes, and the pride of life, is not of the Father, but is of
the world.
17   And the world passeth away, and the lust thereof: but he
that doeth the will of God abideth for ever.

II. Trials

Trials reveal the depth of a person's character and love. The story
of the Willis family is a beautiful illustration of a family coming
through the most extraordinary of trials yet finding peace and
sufficiency in God.

Illustration (trials, excerpt from a tract called "Through the
Flames: The Willis Family Story")

Pastor Duane Scott Willis and his wife Janet dearly loved the
nine children God had given them. But at mid-morning on
November 8, 1994, a fiery auto explosion on I-94 in Milwaukee
claimed the lives of their six youngest. Within hours, the freak
accident had made national and international headlines. From
behind guarded hospital doors came good news concerning Scott
and Janet: their physical recovery from first and second degree
burns would be complete. However, the most astonishing recovery
became apparent as Scott and Janet displayed their emotional
and spiritual stability. Milwaukee, the nation, and even the world

looked on in amazement as eight days later the bereaved couple explained to the media how they could make it through such a sudden and horrific tragedy. The following statements are excerpts from that news conference.

Our God—Our Praise

"Psalm 34 says, 'I will bless the LORD at all times: his praise shall continually be in my mouth. O taste and see that the LORD is good.' Janet and I want to praise and thank God. There is no question in our minds that God is good, and we praise Him in all things. God is a great God."

Our Trial—The Accident

"As far as the accident is concerned, I was looking at the road and was alert. Our little baby was behind us; Ben was behind us on the other side. In the back were the other four children; they were all buckled in. I saw the object (a metal brace, 6″x30″, 30 lbs.). I thought it was one of those blocks that maybe came off a flatbed truck. The car in front of me swerved, and I knew I couldn't miss hitting the object. I thought if I took it on the tire I might roll the car. It was a split-second decision.

"When we hit the object, the rear gas tank exploded, taking the car out of control. I was able to grip the wheel and take the car out of the slide. When we were sliding and the flames were coming around the seat, it was a shock—a surprise—like, 'What is this?' It was just roaring flames coming up on both sides. I was yelling to get out of the car. Janet and I had to consciously put our hands into the flames to unbuckle the seat belts and reach for the door handles.

"Janet fell out the door while the car was still moving. Benny was in the midst of the burning; his clothes were mostly burned off by the time he got out. The five youngest children, who had been asleep, died instantly. No sound was heard by Janet or me as we struggled to get out of the van. An unknown man took his shirt off his back to soak Benny's wounds, and another beat out the burning clothes on Janet's back. Benny died in intensive care around midnight."

Our Children—Our Pain

"We believe children are a heritage of the Lord. We thank God for six precious children: four rascally boys, a sweet girl, so much like her mother, and a little baby just beginning to smile and grow. We understood that they were given of the Lord, and we understood they weren't ours. They were His, and we were stewards of those children. And so God took them back. He is the Giver and Taker of life. We must tell you that we hurt and sorrow as you parents would for your children. The depth of pain is indescribable. The Bible expresses our feelings that we sorrow, but not as those without hope."

Our Confidence—God's Word

"What gives us our firm foundation for our hope is the Bible. The truth of God's Word assures us that Ben, Joe, Sam, Hank, Elizabeth, and Peter are in Heaven with Jesus Christ. We know, based upon the Word of God, where they are. Our strength rests in the Word of God. The Bible is sure and gives us confidence. Everything God promises is true."

Satan was permitted by God to put Job through trials in three different areas: financial trials, family trials, and physical trials.

A. FINANCIAL TRIALS

JOB 1:13–17

13   And there was a day when his sons and his daughters were eating and drinking wine in their eldest brother's house:

14   And there came a messenger unto Job, and said, The oxen were plowing, and the asses feeding beside them:

15   And the Sabeans fell upon them, and took them away; yea, they have slain the servants with the edge of the sword; and I only am escaped alone to tell thee.

16   While he was yet speaking, there came also another, and said, The fire of God is fallen from heaven, and hath burned up the sheep, and the servants, and consumed them; and I only am escaped alone to tell thee.

Lesson Seven—Job—Trusting in Tribulations

17   While he was yet speaking, there came also another, and said, The Chaldeans made out three bands, and fell upon the camels, and have carried them away, yea, and slain the servants with the edge of the sword; and I only am escaped alone to tell thee.

The first area where Satan attacked Job was in his finances. There was a time when Job had "want of nothing." He was very possibly the richest man in the world. In one day, it was all gone: Between the fire, the Sabeans, and the Chaldeans, Job found his financial wealth completely destroyed. This was not enough to cause Job to stop loving and serving His God. But the story goes on:

B.   FAMILY TRIALS

JOB 1:18–19

18   While he was yet speaking, there came also another, and said, Thy sons and thy daughters were eating and drinking wine in their eldest brother's house:
19   And, behold, there came a great wind from the wilderness, and smote the four corners of the house, and it fell upon the young men, and they are dead; and I only am escaped alone to tell thee.

The second attack on Job came through the loss of his family. It is incomprehensible to think of a tornado hitting a home and killing all of one's children, yet this is what happened to Job. Still, through this great trial, he remained faithful. Job knew that his faithfulness to God could not depend on the wellbeing of others. He knew he personally was responsible to serve God. And Job maintained his faith. But Satan wasn't through yet.

C.   PHYSICAL TRIALS

JOB 2:7–10

7   So went Satan forth from the presence of the LORD, and smote Job with sore boils from the sole of his foot unto his crown.

105

8   And he took him a potsherd to scrape himself withal; and he sat down among the ashes.

9   Then said his wife unto him, Dost thou still retain thine integrity? curse God, and die.

10   But he said unto her, Thou speakest as one of the foolish women speaketh. What? shall we receive good at the hand of God, and shall we not receive evil? In all this did not Job sin with his lips.

After devastating Job's finances and his family, Satan moved to take Job's health. The pain of the boils and ultimately the rejection of his wife must have been unbelievably difficult. However, God gives us a statement that is a testimony to Job's life and a challenge to every Christian today: "In all this did not Job sin with his lips."

III. <u>Triumph</u>

It is not unusual to see what appears as tragedy to those around us turn into triumph through the power of our great God. God uses trials and tribulations to shape us, as a sculptor uses a hammer and chisel to shape the stone, or as a potter uses kneading and pressure and heat to make bowls and vases. True quality does not come quickly, easily, or cheaply. Things that are truly valuable often require much time and work for their production. Examples are hand-crafted watches, hand-made shoes, or the work that goes into Steinway pianos.

Illustration (God's detailed working, Steinway pianos):

The Steinway piano has been preferred by keyboard masters such as Rachmaninoff, Horowitz, Van Cliburn, and Liszt—and for good reason. It is a skillfully crafted instrument that produces phenomenal sound. Steinway pianos are built today the same way they were over 150 years ago when Henry Steinway started his business. Two hundred craftsmen and 12,000 parts are required to produce one of these magnificent instruments.

106

Most crucial is the rim-bending process, where 18 layers of maple are bent around an iron press to create the shape of a Steinway grand. Five coats of lacquer are applied and hand-rubbed to give the piano its outer glow. The instrument then goes to the Pounder Room, where each key is tested 10,000 times to ensure quality and durability.

Followers of Jesus Christ are also being "handcrafted." We are pressed and formed and shaped to make us more like Him. We are polished, sometimes in the rubbing of affliction, until we "glow." We are tested in the laboratory of everyday human experience. The process is not always pleasant, but we can persevere with hope, knowing that our lives will increasingly reflect the beauty of holiness to the eternal praise of God. THINK ABOUT IT. Is God bending, shaping, or polishing me right now? What's my attitude: Am I thanking and praising God, or am I complaining about the process? (illustration source unknown)

A. ENLIGHTENMENT

JOB 42:1–6

1 Then Job answered the LORD, and said,

2 I know that thou canst do every thing, and that no thought can be withholden from thee.

3 Who is he that hideth counsel without knowledge? therefore have I uttered that I understood not; things too wonderful for me, which I knew not.

4 Hear, I beseech thee, and I will speak: I will demand of thee, and declare thou unto me.

5 I have heard of thee by the hearing of the ear: but now mine eye seeth thee.

6 Wherefore I abhor myself, and repent in dust and ashes.

Job was "enlightened," which means that he learned from the trials he endured. One of the saddest things that can happen is for someone to endure trials without gaining knowledge from them. God's Word says that one of the ways that we can gain wisdom is through the reproofs of life.

PROVERBS 6:23

23 *For the commandment is a lamp; and the law is light; and reproofs of instruction are the way of life:*

We must ensure that we, like Job, will seek enlightenment from our trials. God allows trials for a reason, and a wise man will learn from the reproofs of life.

B. ENRICHMENT

JOB 42:12–13

12 *So the LORD blessed the latter end of Job more than his beginning: for he had fourteen thousand sheep, and six thousand camels, and a thousand yoke of oxen, and a thousand she asses.*
13 *He had also seven sons and three daughters.*

God's ways are so much better than man's ways. When the story of the trials of Job was finally completed, we discover that in the end God gave him ten more children and that God "blessed the latter end of Job more than his beginning." Job remained faithful and lived to see God's vindication and blessing. We can be assured of the fact that we too can receive enrichment from the Lord when we remain faithful to Him.

Conclusion

Job was a man who endured tremendous trials, and yet through them all he remained faithful to his God. It is interesting to note that Christians today seem ready to walk away from their faith if someone merely mocks them at work. Job was not this type of man. He had a wonderful testimony as he endured his trials, which ultimately led him to reaching a triumph and great blessing of the Lord. The life of Job is a challenge to every believer today to live in a holy and God-pleasing manner no matter what trials may come.

Lesson Seven—Job—Trusting in Tribulations

Study Questions

1. How did God describe Job to Satan?
   God called him "my servant Job...there is none like him in the earth, a perfect and an upright man, one that feareth God, and escheweth evil."

2. Through the workings of Satan, what did Job lose?
   Job lost his oxen, asses, sheep and camels. He lost his children. He lost his health.

3. What did Job say after he had lost his property and his children?
   He said, "Naked came I out of my mother's womb, and naked shall I return thither: the LORD gave, and the LORD hath taken away; blessed be the name of the LORD" (Job 1:21).

4. What has been an example of a great loss in your life, and how did you deal with it?
   Answers will vary.

5. Looking back on this great loss now, do you believe you could you have dealt with it better? How?
   Answers will vary.

6. How can we gain wisdom through our trials?
   Answers will vary, but should include the concept that we need to learn to trust God in difficult circumstances.

7. In what two ways did Job triumph through his trials?
   He was enlightened (he learned) and he was enriched (God blessed him greatly).

109

Lessons from Legends

8. What have you learned from the story of Job that will help you the next time you face a trial?
Answers will vary.

Memory Verses

There was a man in the land of Uz, whose name was Job; and that man was perfect and upright, and one that feared God, and eschewed evil.—JOB 1:1

Then Job arose, and rent his mantle, and shaved his head, and fell down upon the ground, and worshipped, And said, Naked came I out of my mother's womb, and naked shall I return thither: the LORD gave, and the LORD hath taken away; blessed be the name of the LORD.—JOB 1:20–21

LESSON EIGHT

SAMSON
Wasted Potential

Text

JUDGES 16:16–20

16 And it came to pass, when she pressed him daily with her words, and urged him, so that his soul was vexed unto death;

17 That he told her all his heart, and said unto her, There hath not come a razor upon mine head; for I have been a Nazarite unto God from my mother's womb: if I be shaven, then my strength will go from me, and I shall become weak, and be like any other man.

18 And when Delilah saw that he had told her all his heart, she sent and called for the lords of the Philistines, saying, Come up this once, for he hath shewed me all his heart. Then the lords of the Philistines came up unto her, and brought money in their hand.

19 And she made him sleep upon her knees; and she called for a man, and she caused him to shave off the seven locks of his head; and she began to afflict him, and his strength went from him.

20 And she said, The Philistines be upon thee, Samson. And he awoke out of his sleep, and said, I will go out as at other times before, and shake myself. And he wist not that the LORD was departed from him.

Overview

Samson—though born of an answer to prayer, dedicated to God by his parents, and destined to be a deliverer of his people—lived his life in a prideful pleasure-seeking way that led to a shameful and tragic end. It began in his heart, manifested itself in disobedience to his parents and to God, continued as he allowed his fleshly desires to rule over him, and finally culminated in captivity, blindness, and death.

111

Lesson Theme

No matter how strong and good-looking one may be physically, if the heart is not right with God, the inevitable result will be failure. The greatest waste of all may very well be the waste of potential for God.

Lesson Goals

At the conclusion of the lesson, each student should:

1. Understand how Samson's basic attitudes shaped his relationship with his parents and with his God
2. Understand how Samson allowed worldly distractions to rob him of what he could have been for God
3. Decide to focus on obedience to God and to godly authority, and on cultivating a God-honoring attitude

Teaching Outline

Introduction

I. Samson Disobedient
    A. To his parents
    B. To his God

II. Samson Distracted
    A. Past victories
    B. Current temptations

III. Samson Destroyed
    A. Depletion of power
    B. Devastation of potential

Conclusion

LESSON EIGHT

SAMSON
Wasted Potential

Text

JUDGES 16:16–20

16 And it came to pass, when she pressed him daily with her words, and urged him, so that his soul was vexed unto death;

17 That he told her all his heart, and said unto her. There hath not come a razor upon mine head; for I have been a Nazarite unto God from my mother's womb: if I be shaven, then my strength will go from me, and I shall become weak, and be like any other man.

18 And when Delilah saw that he had told her all his heart, she sent and called for the lords of the Philistines, saying, Come up this once, for he hath shewed me all his heart. Then the lords of the Philistines came up unto her, and brought money in their hand.

19 And she made him sleep upon her knees; and she called for a man, and she caused him to shave off the seven locks of his head; and she began to afflict him, and his strength went from him.

20 And she said, The Philistines be upon thee, Samson. And he awoke out of his sleep, and said, I will go out as at other times before, and shake myself. And he wist not that the LORD was departed from him.

113

Introduction

Many people would look at Samson's life and marvel at the victories that were won, but a closer study leaves one pondering the question: "What might have been?" It has been said of Samson that "the Spirit of the Lord came upon him" more times than anyone else in Scripture, and yet, we more vividly remember Samson's end as a blinded and broken prisoner of the enemies of God. He had been born as an answer to prayer, dedicated to the Lord by his godly parents, and was destined to deliver his people from bondage. The process that led him from a birth of promise to a death of disgrace is the subject of our lesson today.

I. Samson Disobedient

As is often the case, troubles begin with a lack of obedience to God. Time after time in Samson's life, we see him failing to obey. And time after time, we see this disobedience bringing with it terrible consequences. Note that Samson's disobedience started early and with his parents. He did not simply wake up one morning and decide to reject all that he had been taught about the Lord. He first was disobedient to his immediate authority.

Illustration (the importance of obedience)

In July 1976, Israeli commandos made a daring raid at an airport in Entebbe, Uganda, during which 103 Jewish hostages were freed. In less than fifteen minutes, the soldiers had killed all seven of the kidnappers and set the captives free.

As successful as the rescue was, however, three of the hostages were killed during the raid. As the commandos entered the terminal, they shouted in Hebrew, "Get down! Crawl!" The Jewish hostages understood and lay down on the floor, while the guerillas, who did not speak Hebrew, were left standing. Quickly the rescuers shot the upright kidnappers.

But two of the hostages hesitated—perhaps to see what was happening—and were also shot down. One young man was lying down and actually stood up when the commandos entered the

114

Lesson Eight—Samson—Potential Wasted

airport. He, too, was shot with the bullets meant for the enemy. Had these three heeded the soldiers' command, they would have been freed with the rest of the captives.

A. To his PARENTS

JUDGES 14:3

3   Then his father and his mother said unto him, Is there never a woman among the daughters of thy brethren, or among all my people, that thou goest to take a wife of the uncircumcised Philistines? And Samson said unto his father, Get her for me; for she pleaseth me well.

Outside of salvation, the most important decision a person can make is whom they will marry. Samson's parents tried to get him to marry someone who believed in the true God, but Samson only wanted someone who would please him.

Samson's parents were godly people (see Judges chapter 13). Samson's very birth was a miracle, and the couple's overriding concern was to please God with the son He had promised to give them. From all appearances, Samson was blessed with good, godly parents who loved him and did whatever they could to train and encourage and provide for Samson's needs and desires. His parents no doubt tried to keep him from going against the precepts of Scripture. Yet, Samson still rejected them and their efforts. God's plan is for children to obey and honor their parents.

EXODUS 20:12

12   Honour thy father and thy mother: that thy days may be long upon the land which the LORD thy God giveth thee.

EPHESIANS 6:1

1   Children, obey your parents in the Lord: for this is right.

COLOSSIANS 3:20

20   Children, obey your parents in all things: for this is well pleasing unto the Lord.

Often a life of rebellion begins with simple disobedience.

B. To his God

JUDGES 13:3–5

3   And the angel of the LORD appeared unto the woman, and said unto her, Behold now, thou art barren, and bearest not: but thou shalt conceive, and bear a son.

4   Now therefore beware, I pray thee, and drink not wine nor strong drink, and eat not any unclean thing:

5   For, lo, thou shalt conceive, and bear a son; and no razor shall come on his head: for the child shall be a Nazarite unto God from the womb: and he shall begin to deliver Israel out of the hand of the Philistines.

NUMBERS 6:6

6   All the days that he [the Nazarite] separateth himself unto the LORD he shall come at no dead body.

JUDGES 14:8–9

8   And after a time he returned to take her, and he turned aside to see the carcase of the lion: and, behold, there was a swarm of bees and honey in the carcase of the lion.

9   And he took thereof in his hands, and went on eating, and came to his father and mother, and he gave them, and they did eat: but he told not them that he had taken the honey out of the carcase of the lion.

DEUTERONOMY 23:21

21   When thou shalt vow a vow unto the LORD thy God, thou shalt not slack to pay it: for the LORD thy God will surely require it of thee; and it would be sin in thee.

Samson again disobeyed the Lord by eating honey out of the lion's carcass. This broke his vow and was in direct disobedience to God's standards for Nazarites. It is also worth noting that in both of these situations, Samson was in places where he should not have been (Philistia and the vineyard). Being in the wrong places led him to engage in wrong actions. We need to learn a strong lesson from this: Sin is a progression, and we will fall in the direction we are leaning.

Lesson Eight—Samson—Potential Wasted

Samson was a God-called man who was privileged to be a judge in Israel. He disobeyed God by walking away from the responsibilities and opportunities that God had given him. As is often the case, this disobedience came because of Samson's lust and pride—the lust of his flesh, the lust of his eyes and his pride of life.

1 JOHN 2:15–17

15   Love not the world, neither the things that are in the world. If any man love the world, the love of the Father is not in him.

16   For all that is in the world, the lust of the flesh, and the lust of the eyes, and the pride of life, is not of the Father, but is of the world.

17   And the world passeth away, and the lust thereof: but he that doeth the will of God abideth for ever.

ROMANS 8:12

12   Therefore, brethren, we are debtors, not to the flesh, to live after the flesh.

JAMES 1:14–15

14   But every man is tempted, when he is drawn away of his own lust, and enticed.

15   Then when lust hath conceived, it bringeth forth sin: and sin, when it is finished, bringeth forth death.

II. Samson <u>Distracted</u>

One of the most important things that God's people can do is to focus on the things that please God.

PHILIPPIANS 3:13–14

13   Brethren, I count not myself to have apprehended: but this one thing I do, forgetting those things which are behind, and reaching forth unto those things which are before,

14   I press toward the mark for the prize of the high calling of God in Christ Jesus.

117

Lessons from Legends

HEBREWS 12:1–2

1   Wherefore seeing we also are compassed about with so great a cloud of witnesses, let us lay aside every weight, and the sin which doth so easily beset us, and let us run with patience the race that is set before us,

2   Looking unto Jesus the author and finisher of our faith; who for the joy that was set before him endured the cross, despising the shame, and is set down at the right hand of the throne of God.

1 CORINTHIANS 9:25–27

25   And every man that striveth for the mastery is temperate in all things. Now they do it to obtain a corruptible crown; but we an incorruptible.

26   I therefore so run, not as uncertainly; so fight I, not as one that beateth the air:

27   But I keep under my body, and bring it into subjection: lest that by any means, when I have preached to others, I myself should be a castaway.

Time after time Samson lost his focus; without that focus, he squandered opportunities and never claimed victories that were his for the taking.

Illustration (focus)

There is an interesting story that is told about the legendary baseball players Hank Aaron and Yogi Berra. Hank Aaron of the Milwaukee Braves was new to the Major Leagues but was already one of the best home run hitters in baseball. Yogi Berra was the colorful veteran catcher for the New York Yankees, and their teams were playing each other in the World Series.

Berra was famous for distracting batters with his constant chatter. Hank Aaron stepped up to the plate, and Berra started in on him: "Hank, you're holding the bat all wrong! You're supposed to hold it so that you can read the label."

Aaron, focused on the pitcher, ignored Berra, and then proceeded to hit the first pitch over the fence into the left field bleachers for a home run. He ran around the bases, came back to home plate, and said to Yogi: "I didn't come up here to read."

A. PAST VICTORIES

The Apostle Paul characterized himself as "forgetting those things which are behind, and reaching forth unto those things which are before" (Philippians 3:13). People who dwell on the past often miss opportunities that are at hand. If Samson had not returned to see the lion he had killed, he would never have seen the honey nor broken his vow to God. He chose to go back to his former sin—not intending to partake in it, but to glory in it for just a moment. This led to a huge failure in his life.

B. CURRENT TEMPTATIONS

When Samson met Delilah, he had a choice. He could flee temptation, as Joseph fled from Potiphar's wife (Genesis 39:7–12), or he could pursue it. Samson gave in to the temptation, and it ultimately led to his destruction.

He went back to the vineyard to take a woman he was not supposed to marry, simply because she pleased him. She did not please God, but that was not a consideration with Samson. As we live our lives today, what pleases us really does not matter—it needs to be all about what pleases God.

III. Samson Destroyed

Illustration (We often fail to consider the gradual, cumulative effect of sin in our lives.)

In St. Louis in 1984, an unemployed cleaning woman noticed a few bees buzzing around the attic of her home. Since there were only a few, she made no effort to deal with them. Over the summer the bees continued to fly in and out the attic vent while the woman remained unconcerned, unaware of the growing city of bees.

The whole attic became a hive, and the ceiling of the second-floor bedroom finally caved in under the weight of hundreds of pounds of honey and thousands of angry bees. While the woman escaped serious injury, she was unable to repair the damage of her accumulated neglect.

Illustration (The following anecdote is by J. Wilbur Chapman)

"I was once a pastor at Schuylerville, New York, where on the Burgoyne surrender grounds stands a celebrated monument. It is beautiful to look upon. On one side of it in a niche is General Schuyler, and on the other side, if I remember correctly, General Gates; on the third, in the same sort of a niche, another distinguished general [General Daniel Morgan] is to be seen, but on the fourth the niche is vacant. When I asked the reason I was told that 'It is the niche which might have been filled by Benedict Arnold had he not been a traitor.'"

"The Saratoga Monument commemorates the surrender of the British Army under the command of General John Burgoyne to General Horatio Gates, commander of the America forces on 17 October 1777 following the battles of Saratoga. The battles and subsequent surrender are considered a turning point in the American Revolution by leading to French support and the hope of ultimate victory." The monument was completed in 1887, and the fourth niche remains vacant to this day. (http://www.revolutionaryday.com/usroute4/schuylerville/default.htm)

A. Depletion of power

Judges 16:20

20 And she said, The Philistines be upon thee, Samson. And he awoke out of his sleep, and said, I will go out as at other times before, and shake myself. And he wist not that the LORD was departed from him.

The saddest moments of Samson's life, from some perspectives, were his final days when he was blinded and grinding for the Philistines like an animal. However, long before that, when Samson had risen up to fight the Philistines, he had "wist (known) not that the LORD was departed from him." Believers need to understand that our sins separate us from God and therefore deprive us of His fellowship, His power, and His blessing.

Lesson Eight—Samson—Potential Wasted

ISAIAH 59:1–2

1   Behold, the LORD's hand is not shortened, that it cannot save; neither his ear heavy, that it cannot hear:

2   But your iniquities have separated between you and your God, and your sins have hid his face from you, that he will not hear.

To be separated from God by our own sin and stubbornness is indescribably sad, because God is our source of victory and God is our source of strength. Bob Jones, Sr., often said, "Don't sacrifice the permanent on the altar of the immediate." In other words, ignore any advice that encourages you to "live for the moment" with no thought of the consequences down the road. For the sake of a few brief moments of prideful pleasure, Samson lost everything that God had offered him.

B. DEVASTATION OF POTENTIAL

From the circumstances of his birth and the solicitude of his godly parents, it is evident that God had great plans for Samson. And God did use him to win some victories; in fact, the Bible says that he killed more Philistines in his death than he had during his life. But there is no doubt that much of Samson's potential was wasted by his own foolishness and self-indulgence. He cared only about himself and his own pleasures.

Conclusion

Remember the words of poet John Greenleaf Whittier, "For of all sad words of tongue or pen, the saddest are these: 'It might have been'!" Just think of what might have been: After the death of Samson, only one more judge ruled over the nation of Israel before the kings came to power. His name was Samuel. There was, however, a stark difference between Samson and Samuel. Samuel said to the Lord, "Speak; for thy servant heareth" (1 Samuel 3:10).

But Samson, rather than seeking God's will, had said to his parents, "Get her for me; for she pleaseth me well" (Judges 14:3). The difference between these statements should be a challenge to every believer. Are we seeking what we desire for ourselves, or are we waiting for the direction of the Lord?

Lesson Eight—Samson—Potential Wasted

Study Questions

1. Give examples of Samson's disobedience.
   Samson disobeyed his parents by taking a woman from the heathen Philistines. Samson disobeyed God by breaking the vow he had taken as a Nazarite.

2. Give some examples of Bible verses that guide us in the attitude we should have toward our parents.
   Possible answers: "Honour thy father and thy mother: that thy days may be long upon the land which the LORD thy God giveth thee."—EXODUS 20:12

   "Children, obey your parents in the Lord: for this is right." —EPHESIANS 6:1

   "Children, obey your parents in all things: for this is well pleasing unto the Lord."—COLOSSIANS 3:20

3. What attitudes in Samson's heart led him to disobey his parents and his God?
   Samson disobeyed out of his lust and pride.

4. In general, on what do God's people need to focus?
   God's people need to focus on the things that please God.

5. Why did Samson say he wanted Delilah?
   Samson said, "She pleaseth me well," and ignored the fact that she did not please God.

6. In what area or areas of your life is your focus on pleasing yourself rather than pleasing God?
   Answers will vary.

123

Lessons from Legends

7. What did Dr. Bob Jones, Sr. mean when he said, "Don't sacrifice the permanent on the altar of the immediate"? *Ignore any advice that encourages you to "live for the moment" with no thought of the consequences down the road.*

8. What effect does our sin have on our relationship with God? *Our sins separate us from God and deprive us of His fellowship, His power, and His blessing.*

Memory Verse

And she said, The Philistines be upon thee, Samson. And he awoke out of his sleep, and said, I will go out as at other times before, and shake myself. And he wist not that the LORD *was departed from him.*—JUDGES 16:20

LESSON NINE

CENTURION
The Man Who Amazed Jesus

Text

LUKE 7:6–9

6   *Then Jesus went with them. And when he was now not far from the house, the centurion sent friends to him, saying unto him, Lord, trouble not thyself: for I am not worthy that thou shouldest enter under my roof:*

7   *Wherefore neither thought I myself worthy to come unto thee: but say in a word, and my servant shall be healed.*

8   *For I also am a man set under authority, having under me soldiers, and I say unto one, Go, and he goeth; and to another, Come, and he cometh; and to my servant, Do this, and he doeth it.*

9   *When Jesus heard these things, he marvelled at him, and turned him about, and said unto the people that followed him, I say unto you, I have not found so great faith, no, not in Israel.*

Overview

Of all the people Jesus encountered during His time here on the earth, only a few really impressed Him. One of these was a Roman centurion who displayed such generosity, humility, and faith that the Bible says Jesus "marvelled." In our lesson today, we will take a closer look at each of these qualities, see how this centurion exemplified them, and learn how we can cultivate these traits in our own lives.

Lesson Theme

God's generosity to us should encourage us to be a giving people. God's greatness should prompt us to humility and a realization of

125

our own unworthiness. God's trustworthiness should lead us to a life of walking by faith.

Lesson Goals

At the conclusion of the lesson, each student should:

1. Understand the concepts of generosity, humility, and faith
2. Understand how the centurion displayed these qualities
3. Understand how we can cultivate and display these qualities in our own lives

Teaching Outline

Introduction

I. Great Generosity
   A. Generosity to his servant
   B. Generosity to the Jews

II. Great Humility
   A. Not worthy to come to Jesus
   B. Not worthy for Jesus to come to him

III. Great Faith
   A. Great faith shown
   B. Great faith seen

Conclusion

LESSON NINE

CENTURION
The Man Who Amazed Jesus

Text

LUKE 7:6–9

6 *Then Jesus went with them. And when he was now not far from the house, the centurion sent friends to him, saying unto him, Lord, trouble not thyself: for I am not worthy that thou shouldest enter under my roof:*

7 *Wherefore neither thought I myself worthy to come unto thee: but say in a word, and my servant shall be healed.*

8 *For I also am a man set under authority, having under me soldiers, and I say unto one, Go, and he goeth; and to another, Come, and he cometh; and to my servant, Do this, and he doeth it.*

9 *When Jesus heard these things, he marvelled at him, and turned him about, and said unto the people that followed him, I say unto you, I have not found so great faith, no, not in Israel.*

Introduction

There are only two times that the Bible says that Jesus Christ marvelled. We find that the first time was in Mark 6, when the

Lord marvelled at the lack of belief of the citizens of Nazareth. He found it astounding that people could see so much and still be so blinded and refuse to believe. They had every reason to believe, and yet chose not to believe.

The second time that Jesus marvelled is found in Luke 7. This is the story of a Roman centurion who had such great faith that Jesus was amazed. What was it about this man that made Jesus stop and marvel? What are the attributes found in the centurion's life that we can seek to emulate?

I. Great Generosity

With the financial uncertainty many are facing these days, truly generous people seem to be harder and harder to find. The philosophy of the world has always been, "Look out for Number One," meaning one's self. Those whose focus is on their own personal needs cannot focus on the needs of others. It is even possible to be generous out of selfish motives.

Illustration

One Sunday a pastor told his congregation that the church needed some extra money and asked the people to prayerfully consider giving a little extra in the offering plate. He said that whoever gave the most would be able to pick out three hymns. After the offering plates were passed, the pastor glanced down and noticed that someone had placed a $1,000 bill in the offering. He was so excited that he immediately shared his joy with his congregation and said he'd like to personally thank the person who placed the money in the plate. A very quiet, elderly, saintly lady all the way in the back shyly raised her hand. The pastor asked her to come to the front. Slowly she made her way to the pastor. He told her how wonderful it was that she gave so much and in thanksgiving asked her to pick out three hymns. Her eyes brightened as she looked over the congregation, pointed to the three handsomest men in the building and said, "I'll take him and him and him."

Lesson Nine—Centurion—The Man Who Amazed Jesus

Those who will reach out in generosity to others, out of a heart of love, will find great blessing as a by-product. In other words, the greatest blessing comes not from *seeking* a blessing, but rather from *being* a blessing.

Illustration

Shortly after World War II came to a close, Europe began picking up the pieces. Much of the Old Country had been ravaged by war and was in ruins. Perhaps the saddest sight of all was that of little orphaned children starving in the streets of those war-torn cities. Early one chilly morning an American soldier was making his way back to the barracks in London. As he turned the corner in his jeep, he spotted a little lad with his nose pressed to the window of a pastry shop. Inside the cook was kneading dough for a fresh batch of doughnuts. The hungry boy stared in silence, watching every move. The soldier pulled his jeep to the curb, stopped, got out and walked quietly over to where the little fellow was standing. Through the steamed-up window he could see the mouth-watering morsels as they were being pulled from the oven, piping hot. The boy salivated and released a slight groan as he watched the cook place them onto the glass-enclosed counter ever so carefully. The soldier's heart went out to the nameless orphan as he stood beside him. "Son...would you like some of those?" The boy was startled. "Oh, yeah...I would!" The American stepped inside and bought a dozen, put them in a bag, and walked back to where the lad was standing in the foggy cold of the London morning. He smiled, held out the bag, and said simply: "Here you are." As he turned to walk away, he felt a tug on his coat. He looked back and heard the child ask quietly: "Mister...are you God?" We are never more like God than when we give. "God so loved the world, that he gave..." (from *Improving Your Serve* by Charles R. Swindoll).

A. GENEROSITY TO HIS SERVANT

LUKE 7:2

2   And a certain centurion's servant, who was dear unto him, was sick, and ready to die.

Although the centurion was a Roman, he was willing to humble himself to go to the Jews in order to get to Jesus.

We see in this passage that the servant was dear to his master the centurion. Even though the social status of the centurion was far above that of the servant, he still cared deeply for his servant. God's Word tells us to love the lowly and even the unlovely.

1 Thessalonians 5:14

14 *Now we exhort you, brethren, warn them that are unruly, comfort the feebleminded, support the weak, be patient toward all men.*

Romans 15:1

1 *We then that are strong ought to bear the infirmities of the weak, and not to please ourselves.*

Ephesians 4:32

32 *And be ye kind one to another, tenderhearted, forgiving one another, even as God for Christ's sake hath forgiven you.*

Luke 6:35

35 *But love ye your enemies, and do good, and lend, hoping for nothing again; and your reward shall be great, and ye shall be the children of the Highest: for he is kind unto the unthankful and to the evil.*

The Lord is always pleased when we reach out to help someone in need. When was the last time you went out of your way to express concern for someone who is not as financially or emotionally secure as you are? It is a challenge to believers today to allow people to be dear unto us who might be from a bus route, a lower-income part of town, or in a hospital or convalescent home.

We also see a tremendous lesson here for those who have others who help them. It is very easy to take for granted the support of those around us. Sometimes, as parents or employers, we cease to realize all that those who are under us do to help us. The centurion was obviously acutely aware of

Lesson Nine—Centurion—The Man Who Amazed Jesus

the value of his servant, and as a kind boss, he did everything he could to care for this man under his authority. Have you ever invested so much in simply caring for someone under you?

B. Generosity to the Jews

Luke 7:5

5 *For he loveth our nation, and he hath built us a synagogue.*

Far from resenting the centurion's authority over them, the Jews rather paid tribute to his generosity. This centurion showed love both corporately (to the group) and individually. We see the centurion was the type of man who loved his neighbors (in James 2:8, this is called "the royal law") even though they were not like him or of the same religion. It is amazing to think that this man was willing to build a synagogue for the people who were in subjugation to him. He could have taken the attitude that he owed them nothing; but instead of forcing the Jews to serve him, he took the initiative to serve them.

In both of these instances—in his generosity to his servant and his generosity to the Jews—the centurion was willing to serve. Biblical compassion is not a feeling, but rather an action. Many claim to have compassion on the lost or on those around them, but it is obvious who truly does: they are willing to sacrifice their own pleasure for the sake of doing something to show someone else that they care.

II. Great Humility

One of the single most important principles for the Christian to learn is that God is always pleased with humility.

James 4:6

6 *But he giveth more grace. Wherefore he saith, God resisteth the proud, but giveth grace unto the humble.*

131

1 Peter 5:5

5 *Likewise, ye younger, submit yourselves unto the elder. Yea, all of you be subject one to another, and be clothed with humility: for God resisteth the proud, and giveth grace to the humble.*

The centurion was aware of this truth. He did not come to Jesus and demand His assistance on the grounds of his personal or official authority; he instead acted with extreme humility, as a servant instead of a master.

Illustration

Civil War General George McClellan was put in charge of the great Army of the Potomac, primarily because public opinion was on his side. He enjoyed being told he was a "Young Napoleon." However, history records that his efforts were less than sensational and he was not a great military leader.

One evening President Abraham Lincoln and two of his staff members went to visit McClellan at his home. McClellan was at a wedding. One hour later McClellan appeared and did not even pay attention to the three men awaiting his return.

Later, a servant reported back to the waiting party that McClellan had gone to bed! The President's associates were enraged, but Lincoln merely got up and led the way home. "This is not the time to be making points of etiquette and personal dignity," the President explained. "I would hold McClellan's horse if he will only bring us success."

Illustration

The famous humanitarian Albert Schweitzer was once traveling by train. Some dignitaries came to meet him at the station. First class unloaded. Second class unloaded. They turned to go, certain that he had missed the train. As third class unloaded, off came Dr. Schweitzer. "Why were you riding third class?" Reply: "Because there was no fourth class."

132

Illustration

On his seventieth birthday, pioneer missionary William Carey wrote to one of his sons these words, recorded by Timothy George in "Faithful Witness":

"I am this day seventy years old, a monument of divine mercy and goodness, though on a review of my life I find much, very much, for which I ought to be humbled in the dust; my direct and positive sins are innumerable, my negligence in the Lord's work has been great, I have not promoted his cause, nor sought his glory and honour as I ought, notwithstanding all this, I am spared till now, and am still retained in his work, and I trust I am received into the divine favour through him."

Quotes by Mark Twain:

- The fellow who blows his horn the loudest is usually in the biggest fog.
- Nature never intended for us to pat ourselves on the back. If she had, our hinges would be different.
- Noise proves nothing. Often a hen who has merely laid an egg cackles as if she had laid an asteroid.

Miscellaneous Quotes:

- The fellow who brags about how smart he is wouldn't if he were.
- The only time you should blow your horn is when you're in the band.
- A person interrupts and endangers his climb up the ladder of success when he stops to pat himself on the back.
- The minute a man begins to feel his importance, his friends begin to doubt it.
- Intelligence is like a river, the deeper it flows the less noise it makes.

A. Not worthy to come to Jesus

Luke 7:3

3   And when he heard of Jesus, he sent unto him the elders of the Jews, beseeching him that he would come and heal his servant.

Luke 7:7

7   Wherefore neither thought I myself worthy to come unto thee: but say in a word, and my servant shall be healed.

The centurion knew that Jesus had the answers to his worries. We need to realize that Christ had the answers then and He still has the answers now. We see here that the centurion "beseeched" Jesus to come and heal his servant. *Beseech* means "desire, entreat, pray." This centurion was literally begging Christ to heal his servant.

It is also interesting to note that this man, in his humility, did not even go to the Master himself because he did not feel worthy to come into His presence with such a request. Believers today need to realize the truth that we, of ourselves, are not worthy to come before God. We often speak of Christ's command for us to come boldly before Him, but we must be careful to not forget our own wretchedness before Christ washed us. Yes, we may come boldly, but at the same time we come badly in need of His mercy and grace.

Hebrews 4:16

16   Let us therefore come boldly unto the throne of grace, that we may obtain mercy, and find grace to help in time of need.

B. Not worthy for Jesus to come to him

Luke 7:6–7

6   Then Jesus went with them. And when he was now not far from the house, the centurion sent friends to him, saying unto him, Lord, trouble not thyself: for I am not worthy that thou shouldest enter under my roof:

7   Wherefore neither thought I myself worthy to come unto thee...

The Lord decided to go the centurion's house to heal the servant. There are three truths of which we should be aware:

1. The centurion's recognition that Jesus had the ability to heal his servant
2. The centurion's realization that the Lord did not need to be physically present to perform His miraculous workings
3. The centurion's regard of his own unworthiness

These three principles all apply to believers today. We must understand that the Lord can do whatever needs to be done, that we need to submit to His methodology and His schedule, and that we must never presume that we deserve any of His blessings.

MATTHEW 28:18

18   And Jesus came and spake unto them, saying, All power is given unto me in heaven and in earth.

JOHN 6:6

6   And this he said to prove him: for he himself knew what he would do.

LAMENTATIONS 3:22

22   It is of the LORD's mercies that we are not consumed, because his compassions fail not.

EPHESIANS 2:8–9

8   For by grace are ye saved through faith; and that not of yourselves: it is the gift of God:

9   Not of works, lest any man should boast.

III.   Great <u>Faith</u>

God makes it clear: He requires faith; He is pleased by faith, and He blesses faith. Time after time throughout Scripture, we see people who were willing to walk by faith. Read through Hebrews chapter 11, which has been called the "Hall of Faith."

135

Hebrews 11:1–2

1   Now faith is the substance of things hoped for, the evidence of things not seen.

2   For by it the elders obtained a good report.

And then the writer begins to "call the roll" and describe their deeds of faith: Abel, Enoch, Noah, Abraham, Isaac, Jacob, Joseph, Moses, and the list goes on. Through the examples in this chapter, we see that faith is much more than belief: it is *taking action* based upon that belief.

In the Christian life, there are really only two choices as to how we are going to live: we can walk by faith, or we can walk by sight. Abraham walked by faith; Jacob and Lot often walked by sight. We cannot ever please God unless we are living by faith.

Romans 14:23

23   ...whatsoever is not of faith is sin.

2 Corinthians 5:7

7   (For we walk by faith, not by sight:)

Without faith, in fact, it is *impossible* to please God. Faith in God is absolutely necessary as a foundation in our day-to-day relationship with Him.

Hebrews 11:6

6   But without faith it is impossible to please him: for he that cometh to God must believe that he is, and that he is a rewarder of them that diligently seek him.

Illustration

Isaac Rankin says that just outside his window is a large wire which carries a heavy current of electricity for light and power. It is carefully insulated at every pole and is out of common reach. "However," he says, "if I could lean out far enough to grasp it, death would be as swift as a lightning stroke. Yet the doves in my neighborhood suffer no harm when they perch on it. They fly from my windowsill, where I sometimes feed them, and preen in safety and contentment on the cables. The secret is that when they

Lesson Nine—Centurion—The Man Who Amazed Jesus

contact that wire, they touch nothing else. My danger would be that should I attempt to reach out and do so, the walls of my house would act as a ground, and the current would turn my body into a channel through which the electricity would flow in damaging power. Because they rest wholly upon the wire, they are unharmed. So God would have us seek our safety in complete surrender to His power and love. It is when we reach one hand to Him while still holding fast to some forbidden thing with the other that we are in danger."

Illustration

Everyone knows how to have faith. We do it all the time in countless ways. When I get in a car and turn the ignition key I have faith that my car will start. When I pick up a ball point pen and press it down on a sheet of paper, I'm exercising faith in the ability of that pen to write. When I sit down to eat and put my wife's cooking into my mouth I am exercising faith that my wife hasn't poisoned the food. Day by day, in countless ways we exercise faith in the people or things around us. Likewise, when Jesus asks us to have faith in Him, He is only asking us to do what is natural for us to do.—Bill Gordon (Fredericksburg Bible Illustrator Supplements)

A. Great faith shown

Luke 7:7

7 Wherefore neither thought I myself worthy to come unto thee: but say in a word, and my servant shall be healed.

It is such a blessing to see that the centurion believed in the power of the spoken Word of God. We are reminded that God spoke the very universe and everything in it into existence.

Genesis 1:1–3, 6, 9, 11

1 In the beginning God created the heaven and the earth.

2 And the earth was without form, and void; and darkness was upon the face of the deep. And the Spirit of God moved upon the face of the waters.

*3 **And God said,** Let there be light: and there was light.*

137

6 **And God said,** *Let there be a firmament in the midst of the waters, and let it divide the waters from the waters.*

9 **And God said,** *Let the waters under the heaven be gathered together unto one place, and let the dry land appear: and it was so.*

11 **And God said,** *Let the earth bring forth grass, the herb yielding seed, and the fruit tree yielding fruit after his kind, whose seed is in itself, upon the earth: and it was so.*

JOHN 1:1–3
1 *In the beginning was the Word, and the Word was with God, and the Word was God.*

2 *The same was in the beginning with God.*

3 *All things were made by him; and without him was not any thing made that was made.*

We should have this same belief in the written Word, for it has the same power.

EXODUS 31:18
18 *And he gave unto Moses, when he had made an end of communing with him upon mount Sinai, two tables of testimony, tables of stone, written with the finger of God.*

HEBREWS 4:12
12 *For the word of God is quick, and powerful, and sharper than any twoedged sword, piercing even to the dividing asunder of soul and spirit, and of the joints and marrow, and is a discerner of the thoughts and intents of the heart.*

B. GREAT FAITH SEEN

LUKE 7:9
9 *When Jesus heard these things, he marvelled at him, and turned him about, and said unto the people that followed him, I say unto you, I have not found so great faith, no, not in Israel.*

The centurion stands as a bright and shining light here in Luke 7. Jesus recognized the great faith of this man, and as

He called attention to this faith, all who were there came to recognize it as well.

As we live by faith, God will use us to have an impact on the lives of others. As the centurion did so many centuries ago, believers today need to put their faith in Christ alone to meet all of their needs. The psalmist said in Psalm 20:7, "Some trust in chariots, and some in horses; but we will remember the name of the LORD our God." As Jesus asked His disciples in Luke 8:25, so He asks us today, "Where is your faith?"

Conclusion

More than ever before, we need people today who will show the world a spirit of generosity, a life of humility, and a walk of faith. Do you want to be different for Christ? Here is a good start! There is no doubt that these attributes will bring amazement to a world that is often selfish, proud, and dependent upon sight.

Study Questions

1. What three major characteristics of the centurion did we study in this lesson?
   We studied the centurion's generosity, his humility, and his faith.

2. In what ways did the centurion demonstrate his generosity?
   He sent for Jesus on behalf of his servant. He had built a synagogue for the Jews.

3. In what ways did the centurion demonstrate his humility?
   He felt unworthy to come to Jesus himself, but sent the Jews to Him. He felt unworthy to have Jesus come to his house to heal the servant, but said that Jesus could simply heal him from where He was.

4. Complete this sentence: "Without _____, it is impossible to please God." What verse tells us this?
   *"Without **faith**, it is impossible to please God."—Hebrews 11:6*

5. How did the centurion demonstrate his faith?
   He demonstrated his faith by expressing the certainty that Jesus could heal his servant, and didn't even have to go to him personally to heal him.

6. In what specific ways can you show a spirit of generosity this week?
   Answers will vary.

7. In what specific ways can you show a spirit of humility this week?
   Answers will vary.

Lesson Nine—Centurion—The Man Who Amazed Jesus

8.   In what specific ways can you demonstrate faith this week: not merely believing, but acting upon the belief?
Answers will vary.

Memory Verse

When Jesus heard these things, he marvelled at him, and turned him about, and said unto the people that followed him, I say unto you, I have not found so great faith, no, not in Israel.—LUKE 7:9

LESSON TEN

ESTHER
Found Faithful

Text

ESTHER 4:13–17

13   Then Mordecai commanded to answer Esther, Think not with thyself that thou shalt escape in the king's house, more than all the Jews.

14   For if thou altogether holdest thy peace at this time, then shall there enlargement and deliverance arise to the Jews from another place; but thou and thy father's house shall be destroyed: and who knoweth whether thou art come to the kingdom for such a time as this?

15   Then Esther bade them return Mordecai this answer,

16   Go, gather together all the Jews that are present in Shushan, and fast ye for me, and neither eat nor drink three days, night or day: I also and my maidens will fast likewise; and so will I go in unto the king, which is not according to the law: and if I perish, I perish.

17   So Mordecai went his way, and did according to all that Esther had commanded him.

Overview

Through the malicious workings of a jealous and wicked man, God's people found themselves in great danger. But God in His providence had already placed a special young lady in a key position. Queen Esther courageously trusted in the Lord and interceded for her people, and God worked a great miracle of deliverance.

143

Lesson Theme

"For such a time as this," God had a vital place and a special task for a prepared person. We may not know why God has put us where we are, but we can be assured that God has a good reason. Our responsibility is, as was Esther's, to be prepared and submissive to God so that He can use us as He desires.

Lesson Goals

At the conclusion of the lesson, each student should:

1. Understand the danger that God's people and Esther herself faced
2. Appreciate the faith and courage Esther showed in the actions she took
3. Determine to be found faithful both now and in the future

Teaching Outline

Introduction

    I. Tough Times
        A. Uncertain future
        B. Unapproachable king

    II. Tender Traits
        A. Cared enough to speak
        B. Cared enough to fast and pray

    III. Triumphant Testimony
        A. Esther
        B. Mordecai
        C. People

Conclusion

LESSON TEN

ESTHER
Found Faithful

Text

ESTHER 4:13–17

13   Then Mordecai commanded to answer Esther, Think not with thyself that thou shalt escape in the king's house, more than all the Jews.

14   For if thou altogether holdest thy peace at this time, then shall there enlargement and deliverance arise to the Jews from another place; but thou and thy father's house shall be destroyed: and who knoweth whether thou art come to the kingdom for such a time as this?

15   Then Esther bade them return Mordecai this answer,

16   Go, gather together all the Jews that are present in Shushan, and fast ye for me, and neither eat nor drink three days, night or day: I also and my maidens will fast likewise; and so will I go in unto the king, which is not according to the law: and if I perish, I perish.

17   So Mordecai went his way, and did according to all that Esther had commanded him.

145

Introduction

God's Word goes to great lengths to show us that faithfulness is not a trait important only to prophets and preachers. Esther is a beautiful illustration of one who began as a common person and showed herself to be faithful in the direst of circumstances. The situations she faced and overcame through faith, we as believers may encounter as well. Esther's responses are certainly worthy case studies from which we can glean great encouragement and helpful principles.

I. Tough Times

Illustration

Some of you may be old enough to remember the Great Depression, or have heard your parents or grandparents talk about it. For a period of several years, it seemed as though conditions in America kept getting worse and worse every month. The following passage is from the World Book Encyclopedia, 2001 edition, article "Great Depression," contributed by Robert Sobel, Ph.D.

"From 1930 to 1933, prices of industrial stocks fell about 80 percent. Banks and individuals with investments in the stock market lost large sums. Banks had also loaned money to many people who could not repay it. The deepening depression forced large numbers of people to withdraw their savings. Banks had great difficulty meeting the withdrawals, which came at a time when the banks were unable to collect on many loans. Between January 1930 and March 1933, about 9,000 banks failed. The bank failures wiped out the savings of millions of people....

"In 1925, about 3 percent of the nation's workers were unemployed. The unemployment rate reached about 9 percent in 1930 and about 25 percent—or about 13 million persons—in 1933. Many people who kept or found jobs had to take salary cuts. In 1932, wage cuts averaged about 18 percent. Many people, including college graduates, felt lucky to find any job. In 1932, the New York City Police Department estimated that 7,000 persons over the age of 17 shined shoes for a living. A popular song of the 1930s called "Brother, Can You Spare a Dime?" expressed the nationwide despair....

"Human suffering became a reality for millions of Americans as the depression continued. Many died of disease resulting from malnutrition. Thousands lost their home because they could not pay the mortgage. In 1932, at least 25,000 families and more than 200,000 young people wandered through the country seeking food, clothing, shelter, and a job. Many youths traveled in freight trains and lived near train yards in camps called hobo jungles....

"The homeless, jobless travelers obtained food from welfare agencies or religious missions in towns along the way. Most of their meals consisted of soup, beans, or stew and had little nourishment. The travelers begged for food or stole it if they could not get something to eat in any other way. Sometimes they ate scraps of food from garbage cans....

"Many people who lost their home remained in the community. Some crowded into the home of a relative. Others moved to a shabby section of town and built shacks from flattened tin cans and old crates. Groups of these shacks were called Hoovervilles, a name that reflected the people's anger and disappointment at President Hoover's failure to end the depression....

"Peggy Terry, who grew up in Oklahoma during the depression, recalled a visit to a Hooverville in Oklahoma City: 'Here were all these people living in old rusted-out car bodies. ... One family...[was] living in a piano box. This wasn't just a little section; this was maybe 10 miles wide and 10 miles long. People living in whatever they could junk together....'

"Severe droughts and dust storms hit parts of the Midwest and Southwest during the 1930s. The afflicted region became known as the Dust Bowl, and thousands of farm families there were wiped out. Many farmers went to the fertile agricultural areas of California to look for work. Most who found jobs had to work as fruit or vegetable pickers for extremely low wages. The migrant families crowded into shacks near the fields or camped outdoors. John Steinbeck's famous novel *The Grapes of Wrath* (1939) describes the hardships some migrant families faced during the depression."

A. Uncertain future

Esther 3:8–9

8 *And Haman said unto king Ahasuerus, There is a certain people scattered abroad and dispersed among the people in all the provinces of thy kingdom; and their laws are diverse from all people; neither keep they the king's laws: therefore it is not for the king's profit to suffer them.*

9 ***If it please the king, let it be written that they may be destroyed****: and I will pay ten thousand talents of silver to the hands of those that have the charge of the business, to bring it into the king's treasuries.*

Life often does not go as planned. It was said in a poem by Robert Burns, "the best laid plans of mice and men often go awry" (paraphrased). While this certainly seemed to be the case in Esther's life, the sovereignty of God made sure that this was also the case for Haman.

Satan will often attack and try to harm God's people. Here we find the Jewish people being threatened with their very destruction, but Esther did not flee; she became a vessel that God could use.

B. Unapproachable king

Esther 4:11

11 ***All the king's servants, and the people of the king's provinces, do know, that whosoever, whether man or woman, shall come unto the king into the inner court, who is not called, there is one law of his to put him to death****, except such to whom the king shall hold out the golden sceptre, that he may live: but I have not been called to come in unto the king these thirty days.*

It is important to understand that God is greater than any king, president, or prime minister. A great old preacher by the name of Dr. Harold Sightler was known to say, "If God is in it, it will work." In the story of Esther—although it has been noted many times that the name of God appears nowhere in the book—her older cousin and guardian Mordecai was confident that God was going to preserve His people somehow (4:14). While the world would think the king unapproachable, she, after being instructed by her spiritual authority, was willing to approach him. The Lord is looking for people today who are willing to attempt for God things that the world says are impossible.

II. <u>Tender</u> Traits

It is always a blessing to see someone who cares enough to make a difference. It is obvious that Esther cared deeply for the safety and security of her people. In fact, she cared so much that she, like the prophet Jeremiah, could not help but take action.

Illustration

The battle of Fredericksburg, Virginia, during the Civil War was basically a one-sided slaughter. The Army of Northern Virginia, commanded by General Robert E. Lee, had made their stand just west of the Rappahannock River at Fredericksburg with strong positions behind a stone wall and upon Marye's Heights behind the wall. As many as thirteen separate Union attacks had been hurled against that wall and that hill, and all had been repulsed with heavy casualties. All night thousands of wounded and helpless men lay on the open field, moaning and begging for any kind of relief. One Confederate soldier, Sergeant Richard Kirkland of the 2nd South Carolina Volunteers, sought out his commanding officer and asked for permission to carry water to the suffering enemy soldiers. General Kershaw feared that Kirkland would be killed, but also trusted that God would honor and protect such a noble deed. With that, Kirkland gathered all of the canteens he could carry and climbed over the wall out onto the previous day's battlefield. For well over an hour he ministered to his suffering foes as both armies watched in amazement and admiration. Not a shot was fired at him, and when he had done all he could he simply returned to his post and once again took his place in the line. Today a statue depicting Kirkland's compassion stands near the battlefield's visitor center. The fighting men on both sides of the line called him "THE ANGEL OF MARYE'S HEIGHTS."

A. CARED ENOUGH TO SPEAK

ESTHER 4:14

14 *For if thou altogether holdest thy peace at this time, then shall there enlargement and deliverance arise to the Jews from another place; but thou and thy father's house shall be destroyed: and who knoweth whether thou art come to the kingdom for such a time as this?*

ESTHER 8:3

3 *And Esther spake yet again before the king, and fell down at his feet, and besought him with tears to put away the mischief of Haman the Agagite, and his device that he had devised against the Jews.*

Although it has been said that silence is golden, it is also true that at times silence is cowardice. Mordecai urged Esther not to hold her peace in this crisis. He challenged Esther with the thought that God had her there for "such a time as this."

B. CARED ENOUGH TO FAST AND PRAY

ESTHER 4:16

16 *Go, gather together all the Jews that are present in Shushan, and fast ye for me, and neither eat nor drink three days, night or day: I also and my maidens will fast likewise; and so will I go in unto the king, which is not according to the law: and if I perish, I perish.*

Esther knew that she had to speak up for her people, but she also knew that spiritual preparation had to be made first. God's Word says that certain things only come about by fasting and prayer.

MARK 9:25-29

25 *When Jesus saw that the people came running together, he rebuked the foul spirit, saying unto him, Thou dumb and*

Lesson Ten—Esther—Found Faithful

deaf spirit, I charge thee, come out of him, and enter no more into him.

26 And the spirit cried, and rent him sore, and came out of him: and he was as one dead; insomuch that many said, He is dead.

27 But Jesus took him by the hand, and lifted him up; and he arose.

28 And when he was come into the house, his disciples asked him privately, Why could not we cast him out?

29 And he said unto them, This kind can come forth by nothing, but by prayer and fasting.

Esther, along with her maidens and the Jewish people, fasted and prayed for three days. This is a great challenge to believers today—would we be willing to fast and pray for three days for the salvation of others?

III. Triumphant Testimony

It is exciting and miraculous when God works! It is evident in this case that God, in His sovereignty, turned the heart of the king. Haman, who sought to be the destroyer, ultimately became the destroyed. When God does something wonderful, there are benefits that often affect more than one person.

Illustration

Today great inventors of the past are honored: Morse, Edison, Bell, the Wright Brothers, etc. In their own day, many at first ridiculed them as foolish dreamers. But they persevered and triumphed, and many of them saw the vindication of their efforts and the confounding of their critics.

Illustration

Winston Churchill first became Prime Minister of England at age 66, after a lifetime of overcoming defeats and setbacks. When he

151

Lessons from Legends

died nearly twenty-five years later, millions of people around the world mourned his passing.

A. ESTHER

ESTHER 8:4

4   Then the king held out the golden sceptre toward Esther. So Esther arose, and stood before the king,

ESTHER 7:10

10   So they hanged Haman on the gallows that he had prepared for Mordecai. Then was the king's wrath pacified.

It is easy to see that Esther had been blessed by the Lord as early as chapter 2 verse 15. As the story comes to its conclusion, we see that, first of all, the king held out his golden scepter toward Esther and invited her into his presence. We see Esther asking the king to reverse the letters written by Haman, and God moved the king to tell Esther in verse 7 that he had given Esther the house of Haman and had Haman hanged. The Word of God states that it took the hanging of Haman to pacify the king's wrath.

B. MORDECAI

ESTHER 8:2

2   And the king took off his ring, which he had taken from Haman, and gave it unto Mordecai. And Esther set Mordecai over the house of Haman.

ESTHER 8:15

15   And Mordecai went out from the presence of the king in royal apparel of blue and white, and with a great crown of gold, and with a garment of fine linen and purple: and the city of Shushan rejoiced and was glad.

Esther's guardian Mordecai also came forth triumphant. It is not unusual for people to do right and to think that it is all for naught. Such, undoubtedly, was the case for Mordecai. He

Lesson Ten—Esther—Found Faithful

had saved the king's life and the king appeared to have totally forgotten about it (2:21–23). God, in His time, had Mordecai's actions revealed to the king (6:1–3). Christians need to realize that God's blessings come when God decides the time is right. Sometimes, it is quickly; sometimes one has to wait a lengthy period of time; and sometimes one has to wait until eternity in Heaven, but God is always just, and He promises blessing in exchange for obedience.

After the Jews had been preserved, we see that Mordecai was rewarded by the king with apparel of blue and white, a fine linen garment, and a crown of gold (Esther 8:15).

In the final chapter in the book of Esther, the Bible says that the king advanced Mordecai and allowed him to have more power and might. The final verse of the book reveals that Mordecai was made the second most powerful man in the kingdom, where he was allowed to watch for his people.

C. PEOPLE

ESTHER 8:16–17

16 *The Jews had light, and gladness, and joy, and honour.*

17 *And in every province, and in every city, whithersoever the king's commandment and his decree came, the Jews had joy and gladness, a feast and a good day. And many of the people of the land became Jews; for the fear of the Jews fell upon them.*

The Bible says that there was light and honor for the Jews and then goes on to say that many people were converted to Judaism because of seeing the good hand of God upon His people. What a tremendous challenge for believers today— that people would see God working in us and through us that they too might realize that we are serving the true God.

Conclusion

What an example this great woman Esther is to us today! She, as a woman of God, endured tough times while never failing in staying gracious in her personal life and exuding tender traits which showed her love. And, in the end, she was granted a triumphant testimony by her God. Through whatever life may bring, may we always stay faithful and show love that we also may have triumphant testimonies.

Lesson Ten—Esther—Found Faithful

Study Questions

1. What was Haman's plot?
Haman wanted the Jews to be destroyed, so he persuaded the king to order it to be done.

2. Unless the king granted special mercy, what would happen to someone who came to the king uninvited?
He or she was to be put to death.

3. Who was Esther's spiritual mentor?
Esther's spiritual mentor was her cousin and guardian Mordecai.

4. What three actions did Esther take in attempting to get the decree against her people reversed?
Esther spoke to the king, she fasted, and she prayed.

5. Describe the end of Haman.
Esther revealed Haman's plot to the king, and Haman was hanged on the same gallows he had prepared for Mordecai.

6. How can you exercise boldness for God this week?
Answers will vary, but could include: telling someone about Christ, confronting a friend who is headed for trouble, praying before meals in public, etc.

7. For what special problems in your life would you be willing to fast and pray for a solution?
Answers will vary.

8. Describe a time in your life when God gave you a remarkable or even a miraculous deliverance.
Answers will vary.

155

Memory Verses

Then Mordecai commanded to answer Esther, Think not with thyself that thou shalt escape in the king's house, more than all the Jews. For if thou altogether holdest thy peace at this time, then shall there enlargement and deliverance arise to the Jews from another place; but thou and thy father's house shall be destroyed: and who knoweth whether thou art come to the kingdom for such a time as this?—ESTHER 4:13–14

LESSON ELEVEN

ELISHA
A Double Portion

Text

2 KINGS 2:8–14

8   And Elijah took his mantle, and wrapped it together, and smote the waters, and they were divided hither and thither, so that they two went over on dry ground.

9   And it came to pass, when they were gone over, that Elijah said unto Elisha, Ask what I shall do for thee, before I be taken away from thee. And Elisha said, I pray thee, let a double portion of thy spirit be upon me.

10   And he said, Thou hast asked a hard thing: nevertheless, if thou see me when I am taken from thee, it shall be so unto thee; but if not, it shall not be so.

11   And it came to pass, as they still went on, and talked, that, behold, there appeared a chariot of fire, and horses of fire, and parted them both asunder; and Elijah went up by a whirlwind into heaven.

12   And Elisha saw it, and he cried, My father, my father, the chariot of Israel, and the horsemen thereof. And he saw him no more: and he took hold of his own clothes, and rent them in two pieces.

13   He took up also the mantle of Elijah that fell from him, and went back, and stood by the bank of Jordan;

14   And he took the mantle of Elijah that fell from him, and smote the waters, and said, Where is the LORD God of Elijah? and when he also had smitten the waters, they parted hither and thither: and Elisha went over.

Overview

Elisha was just a simple farm boy who was out in the field plowing when a prophet named Elijah came by and chose him as a protégé and successor. Elisha left the farm and followed the man of God. When the time came for Elijah to leave this world, Elisha was ready

157

and bold enough to ask for a double portion of the spirit that Elijah had. God granted his request, and the power that rested on Elisha was obvious to everyone around him.

Lesson Theme

Elisha showed faithfulness first in his own home and then in the work of God. Elisha showed fervency as he followed God's man and stuck with him to the end. Elisha showed fearlessness as he refused to turn back to the old life and carried on for God, bolstered by a double portion of power. Faithfulness, fervency, fearlessness—a mighty combination that God can use in a wonderful way!

Lesson Goals

At the conclusion of the lesson, each student should:

1. Understand the circumstances of Elisha's call and his willingness to follow
2. Understand the concepts of fervency and fearlessness in relationship to service for God
3. Decide to live his or her life for God with faithfulness, fervency, and fearlessness

Teaching Outline

Introduction

I. Faithful
   A. Faithful in his work
   B. Faithful to his leader

II. Fervent
   A. Fervent to follow the call
   B. Fervent to remain faithful in service

III. Fearless
   A. Fearless decisions
   B. Fearless desires
   C. Fearless declarations

Conclusion

LESSON ELEVEN

ELISHA
A Double Portion

Text

2 KINGS 2:8–14

8   And Elijah took his mantle, and wrapped it together, and smote the waters, and they were divided hither and thither, so that they two went over on dry ground.

9   And it came to pass, when they were gone over, that Elijah said unto Elisha, Ask what I shall do for thee, before I be taken away from thee. And Elisha said, I pray thee, let a double portion of thy spirit be upon me.

10   And he said, Thou hast asked a hard thing: nevertheless, if thou see me when I am taken from thee, it shall be so unto thee; but if not, it shall not be so.

11   And it came to pass, as they still went on, and talked, that, behold, there appeared a chariot of fire, and horses of fire, and parted them both asunder; and Elijah went up by a whirlwind into heaven.

12   And Elisha saw it, and he cried, My father, my father, the chariot of Israel, and the horsemen thereof. And he saw him no more: and he took hold of his own clothes, and rent them in two pieces.

13 He took up also the mantle of Elijah that fell from him, and went back, and stood by the bank of Jordan;

14 And he took the mantle of Elijah that fell from him, and smote the waters, and said, Where is the LORD God of Elijah? and when he also had smitten the waters, they parted hither and thither: and Elisha went over.

Introduction

It is always exciting when something is twice as big or twice as grand as the original. It is not uncommon for someone to ask for a large portion of something they desire. This lesson will introduce us to the prophet Elisha, a man who asked for a double portion. God used Elisha in a unique and powerful way. We can clearly see several aspects in the life of Elisha that we can emulate in our own lives.

I. Faithful

1 KINGS 19:19

19 So he [Elijah] departed thence, and found Elisha the son of Shaphat, who was plowing with twelve yoke of oxen before him, and he with the twelfth: and Elijah passed by him, and cast his mantle upon him.

The Bible asks the rhetorical question "a faithful man who can find?"

PROVERBS 20:6

6 Most men will proclaim every one his own goodness: but a faithful man who can find?

At times, it is very difficult to find a man who is wholly dedicated to what he believes and faithful to his cause even when he is not under any form of supervision. Elisha was, from all evidences in the Bible, one of these few faithful men. The Bible teaches us that

Lesson Eleven—Elisha—A Double Portion

he who is faithful in little will be faithful in much, and as we will discover, this was certainly the case in the life of Elisha.

LUKE 16:10

10 He that is faithful in that which is least is faithful also in much: and he that is unjust in the least is unjust also in much.

Illustration

Evangelist Louis Arnold quoted Paul Harvey about a 73-year-old man who was rescued by friends, just in the nick of time, after being pinned beneath his tractor longer than Jonah was in the belly of the great fish. Although his ordeal took place during a driving rain in a terrible storm, the four days and nights cost him only the amputation of one leg below the knee. It could have cost him his life—and would have, too, had not his friends come looking.

Why did they go to his farm to check? He missed prayer meeting! Not showing up for the least attended service on the church calendar caused those who knew him to realize something must be drastically wrong. His faithfulness to the Lord and His work saved his life.

If you missed prayer meeting, would any come looking for you, fearful that something terrible had happened?

A. FAITHFUL IN HIS WORK

Long before Elisha became a prophet of God, he was faithful in his simple tasks at home. Israel, at this time, was an agrarian society. The first time we read about Elisha, we find he is plowing with twelve yoke of oxen in the field. (Probably this meant that, in addition to his own team, he was overseeing eleven other teams that his servants were handling. One man controlling up to twenty-four oxen attached to one plow does not seem feasible or even possible.) This was not an easy job and this was not a popular job, but it was his job and for this reason, Elisha was faithful to it.

161

B. Faithful to his leader

1 Kings 19:19–21

19 So he departed thence, and found Elisha the son of Shaphat, who was plowing with twelve yoke of oxen before him, and he with the twelfth: and Elijah passed by him, and cast his mantle upon him.

20 And he left the oxen, and ran after Elijah, and said, Let me, I pray thee, kiss my father and my mother, and then I will follow thee. And he said unto him, Go back again: for what have I done to thee?

21 And he returned back from him, and took a yoke of oxen, and slew them, and boiled their flesh with the instruments of the oxen, and gave unto the people, and they did eat. Then he arose, and went after Elijah, and ministered unto him.

In these verses, we also find that Elisha was faithful to obey the commands of his leader. These verses show that Elisha listened to Elijah, followed Elijah, and ministered unto Elijah.

II. Fervent

The word *fervent* refers to the intensity with which we do whatever it is we are doing. One of the things that is readily apparent in the life of Elisha is that he had an intensity to do what he was called to do.

Illustration

"When I was a boy, my father, a baker, introduced me to the wonders of song," tenor Luciano Pavarotti (now deceased) related. "He urged me to work very hard to develop my voice. Arrigo Pola, a professional tenor in my hometown of Modena, Italy, took me as a pupil. I also enrolled in a teachers college. On graduating, I asked my father, 'Shall I be a teacher or a singer?'

"'Luciano,' my father replied, 'if you try to sit on two chairs, you will fall between them. For life, you must choose one chair.'

Lesson Eleven—Elisha—A Double Portion

"I chose one. It took seven years of study and frustration before I made my first professional appearance. It took another seven to reach the Metropolitan Opera. And now I think whether it's laying bricks, writing a book—whatever we choose—we should give ourselves to it. Commitment, that's the key. Choose one chair."

A. FERVENT TO FOLLOW THE CALL

1 KINGS 19:20

20 *And he left the oxen, and ran after Elijah, and said, Let me, I pray thee, kiss my father and my mother, and then I will follow thee. And he said unto him, Go back again: for what have I done to thee?*

The interesting lesson of Elisha's following after the call of the Lord in his life is that he *ran* after Elijah. He did not drag his feet. He did not grouchily surrender to his destiny. He did not bitterly accept his fate. He willingly ran to it and swore his allegiance. This act of running is a sign of a total willingness to follow God's plan, and we see this several other times in the Scriptures. We see that Peter ran to the empty tomb of Jesus; Joseph ran to his brothers; David ran to meet Goliath; Philip ran to catch the Ethiopian eunuch. It would be an exciting thing for God's people to determine to run heartily after God's will today.

B. FERVENT TO REMAIN FAITHFUL IN SERVICE

2 KINGS 2:2–6

2 *And Elijah said unto Elisha, Tarry here, I pray thee; for the LORD hath sent me to Bethel.* **And Elisha said unto him, As the LORD liveth, and as thy soul liveth, I will not leave thee.** *So they went down to Bethel.*

3 *And the sons of the prophets that were at Bethel came forth to Elisha, and said unto him, Knowest thou that the LORD will take away thy master from thy head to day? And he said, Yea, I know it; hold ye your peace.*

163

4   And Elijah said unto him, Elisha, tarry here, I pray thee; for the LORD *hath sent me to Jericho.* **And he said, As the LORD liveth, and as thy soul liveth, I will not leave thee.** *So they came to Jericho.*

5   And the sons of the prophets that were at Jericho came to Elisha, and said unto him, Knowest thou that the LORD *will take away thy master from thy head to day? And he answered, Yea, I know it; hold ye your peace.*

6   And Elijah said unto him, Tarry, I pray thee, here; for the LORD *hath sent me to Jordan.* **And he said, As the LORD liveth, and as thy soul liveth, I will not leave thee.** *And they two went on.*

Often, it does not take a lot for people to be dissuaded from that which they were called to do. In 2 Kings 2:2–6, we see one phrase repeated three times: "I will not leave thee." Even people who were supposed to be spiritual—the sons of the prophets—tried to persuade Elisha to leave Elijah, since the Lord was about to take him away. But Elisha was determined to stick with the man of God all the way, and as the Word of God states it so beautifully, "they two went on." It was evident that they shared a common focus. Are your best friends the kind of people who help you and encourage you to walk with God?

AMOS 3:3
3   Can two walk together, except they be agreed?

PROVERBS 27:17
17   Iron sharpeneth iron; so a man sharpeneth the countenance of his friend.

1 SAMUEL 23:16
16   And Jonathan Saul's son arose, and went to David into the wood, and strengthened his hand in God.

III. Fearless

God has not given His people the spirit of fear, but rather of power (2 Timothy 1:7). Elisha made the decision that he would never return to what had been his occupation. As the songwriter said so eloquently, there was to be "no turning back." He had truly decided to follow Jesus. Elisha understood the principle that the gifts and calling of God are without repentance (Romans 11:29); God had not changed His mind and therefore neither would Elisha. Jesus said, "No man, having put his hand to the plough, and looking back, is fit for the kingdom of God" (Luke 9:62).

Illustration

Chrysostom, a great preacher of the fourth century AD who was labeled "Golden mouthed" and was very popular with people, as well as a brilliant scholar, was bold when it came to condemning sin. He was called before the Emperor, whom he had offended. He threatened Chrysostom with exile unless he apologized. Chrysostom replied, "You cannot exile me because this world is my father's house."

"I will kill you," said the Emperor.

"No, you cannot, because my life is hid with Christ in God."

"I will take away your treasures."

"No, you cannot, for my treasure is in heaven and my heart is there."

The Emperor was furious at this point. "I will drive you away from man and you shall have no friend left."

"No, you cannot, for I have a friend in heaven from whom you cannot separate me.... I defy you; for there is nothing that you can do to hurt me!" (From Henry Hart Milman, "History of Christianity" [New York: Crowell, 1881], 4:144)

Illustration

Peter Cartwright, a nineteenth-century circuit-riding Methodist preacher, was an uncompromising man. One Sunday morning when he was to preach, he was told that General Andrew Jackson was in the congregation, and the preacher was warned not to say anything out of line.

When Cartwright stood to preach, he said, "I understand that Andrew Jackson is here. I have been requested to be guarded in my remarks. Andrew Jackson will go to hell if he doesn't repent."

The congregation was shocked and wondered how the General would respond. After service, General Jackson shook hands with Peter Cartwright and said, "Sir, if I had a regiment of men like you, I could whip the world."

A. FEARLESS DECISIONS

Like Abram who followed the calling of God without knowing where he was going, like Ruth who followed Naomi back to Bethlehem, like the disciples who left their families and occupations to follow Jesus, Elisha fearlessly left the farm to follow the man of God. He showed his determination and seriousness by killing one of his yoke of oxen and allowing his people to eat. He wasn't going to be needing them anymore— from this time forth he was going to be serving God with Elijah and wouldn't be coming back.

1 KINGS 19:20–21

20   And he left the oxen, and ran after Elijah, and said, Let me, I pray thee, kiss my father and my mother, and then I will follow thee. And he said unto him, Go back again: for what have I done to thee?

21   And he returned back from him, and took a yoke of oxen, and slew them, and boiled their flesh with the instruments of the oxen, and gave unto the people, and they did eat. Then he arose, and went after Elijah, and ministered unto him.

Illustration

"In 1519, Capitan Hernando Cortes and a small army left the Spanish held island of Cuba and set out on one of the greatest conquests in the history of the world. Cortes was going to accomplish his goals no matter the consequences.

He put to death some of those who opposed him, got himself appointed Capitan-General in order to get out from under Diego Velazquez's authority, and even destroyed his fleet in an attempt to motivate his men to adapt to his at-all-costs attitude." (www.megaessays.com/viewpaper/100347.html)

What have you and I decided to leave behind for the sake of following the Lord? We're familiar with missionaries who leave their own countries to serve the Lord elsewhere in the world, but in truth we are all called to forsake that which would hinder us from serving God. It may be our material possessions that are holding us back, it may be that we have settled into a "comfort zone" which we are unwilling to leave, it may be that we have some friends who are a bad influence on us. Is God speaking to your heart about something in your life that you would be better off without?

HEBREWS 12:1

1   Wherefore seeing we also are compassed about with so great a cloud of witnesses, let us lay aside every weight, and the sin which doth so easily beset us, and let us run with patience the race that is set before us,

1 TIMOTHY 6:7

7   For we brought nothing into this world, and it is certain we can carry nothing out.

B. FEARLESS DESIRES

2 KINGS 2:9

9   And it came to pass, when they were gone over, that Elijah said unto Elisha, Ask what I shall do for thee, before I be taken away from thee. And Elisha said, I pray thee, let a double portion of thy spirit be upon me.

Much like King Solomon, Elisha had the right desires. When Solomon was asked by God what he would like to have, he told God that above all he desired wisdom (1 Kings 3:5–10). When Elisha was asked by Elijah what he would like to have in his life, he said that he wanted a double portion of God's power. What a bold request from a simple country boy!

Undoubtedly Elisha understood that with God, all things are possible (Mark 10:27). He would go on to do God's work in the same way, and, amazingly, he would go on to do twice the number of the recorded miracles of Elijah. In many ways, he was a beautiful illustration of someone who lived what William Carey said: "Expect great things from God. Attempt great things for God."

C. FEARLESS DECLARATIONS

2 KINGS 2:13–15

13 He took up also the mantle of Elijah that fell from him, and went back, and stood by the bank of Jordan;
14 And he took the mantle of Elijah that fell from him, and smote the waters, and said, Where is the LORD God of Elijah? and when he also had smitten the waters, they parted hither and thither: and Elisha went over.
15 And when the sons of the prophets which were to view at Jericho saw him, they said, The spirit of Elijah doth rest on Elisha. And they came to meet him, and bowed themselves to the ground before him.

Elisha realized from where the power of God came. After the fiery chariot had come and gone, he retrieved the mantle of Elijah. Like his predecessor, he smote the water and most importantly, asked—almost challenged—God to work: "Where is the LORD God of Elijah?" As Paul Harvey would have said, "the rest of the story" is that when the waters had been smitten, "they parted hither and thither: and Elisha went over."

One other thing worth mentioning is that others saw God working in and through Elisha. The very same prophets who had encouraged him to turn aside, now acknowledged that he was truly the man of God, and the Bible states they bowed to the ground before him. This is a great challenge to believers today—that we would live in such a way that people would see that God is working in us and through us.

168

Conclusion

As we seek to learn from the legendary characters of the Bible, Elisha offers us many lessons. He began his ministry as a servant for the man of God. Yet, even in this humble and simple job, Elisha was faithful to every task he had. But he was more than faithful. He was passionate. He was fervent. He gave everything he had to fulfilling his responsibilities, and when trials came, he stood fearlessly. Would to God that Christians would rise up and live today the way this legend lived so long ago!

Lessons from Legends

Study Questions

1. How did Elisha signify his decision to follow the man of God?
    He killed one of his yoke of oxen and fed it to his people, since he wouldn't be needing it anymore.

2. How did Elisha show his fervency and eagerness to follow the man of God?
    The Bible says he ran after Elijah. When the time came for God to take Elijah up, Elisha refused to leave him.

3. What are some things that you have left behind for the Lord?
    Answers will vary, but could include: worldly friends, amusements not pleasing to God, a home or a job.

4. When Elijah asked Elisha what he should do for him before he left, what was Elisha's answer?
    Elisha told Elijah that he wanted a double portion of his spirit.

5. How did Elisha demonstrate his new power from God?
    He took the mantle of Elijah and smote the waters of the Jordan River, and they parted.

6. In what areas of your life do you need to demonstrate more faithfulness?
    Answers will vary.

7. In what areas of your life do you need to demonstrate more fervency?
    Answers will vary.

Lesson Eleven—Elisha—A Double Portion

8. In what areas of your life do you need to demonstrate more fearlessness?
    Answers will vary.

Memory Verses

He took up also the mantle of Elijah that fell from him, and went back, and stood by the bank of Jordan; And he took the mantle of Elijah that fell from him, and smote the waters, and said, Where is the LORD God of Elijah? and when he also had smitten the waters, they parted hither and thither: and Elisha went over.
—2 KINGS 2:13–14

LESSON TWELVE

JOSEPH
Living Like Jesus

Text

GENESIS 50:17–21

17   So shall ye say unto Joseph, Forgive, I pray thee now, the trespass of thy brethren, and their sin; for they did unto thee evil: and now, we pray thee, forgive the trespass of the servants of the God of thy father. And Joseph wept when they spake unto him.

18   And his brethren also went and fell down before his face; and they said, Behold, we be thy servants.

19   And Joseph said unto them, Fear not: for am I in the place of God?

20   But as for you, ye thought evil against me; but God meant it unto good, to bring to pass, as it is this day, to save much people alive.

21   Now therefore fear ye not: I will nourish you, and your little ones. And he comforted them, and spake kindly unto them.

Overview

Joseph played a pivotal role in the history of the Hebrew people. Through many circumstances that were certainly not comfortable for him, God brought Joseph from the status of a favored son, through slavery and unjust imprisonment, to a place of prominence in a foreign country. When famine came to the land of Canaan, Joseph in Egypt became the savior of his family.

Lesson Theme

All of us face discouraging circumstances in our lives. The important thing is not so much what happens to us, but rather how we deal with them. In Joseph we see a wonderful example of

173

a man who remained faithful through his trials and was rewarded by God with great usefulness and blessing.

Lesson Goals

At the conclusion of the lesson, each student should:

1. Understand the basic chronology of the life of Joseph
2. Understand how he remained faithful through each trial
3. Decide to remain faithful to God no matter what adverse circumstances life may bring

Teaching Outline

Introduction

   I. Faithful as a Son
     A. Loved by his father
     B. Hated by his brothers
     C. Obedient to his call

  II. Faithful as a Servant
     A. Potiphar's house
     B. Pharaoh's prison
     C. People of Egypt

 III. Faithful as a Sovereign
     A. Forgiving sovereign
     B. Saving sovereign

Conclusion

LESSON TWELVE

JOSEPH
Living Like Jesus

Text

GENESIS 50:17–21

17 So shall ye say unto Joseph, Forgive, I pray thee now, the trespass of thy brethren, and their sin; for they did unto thee evil: and now, we pray thee, forgive the trespass of the servants of the God of thy father. And Joseph wept when they spake unto him.

18 And his brethren also went and fell down before his face; and they said, Behold, we be thy servants.

19 And Joseph said unto them, Fear not: for am I in the place of God?

20 But as for you, ye thought evil against me; but God meant it unto good, to bring to pass, as it is this day, to save much people alive.

21 Now therefore fear ye not: I will nourish you, and your little ones. And he comforted them, and spake kindly unto them.

Introduction

In all the annals of Scripture, there is probably no greater type of the Lord Jesus Christ than Joseph. The life of Joseph speaks to

175

believers in a wide variety of walks of life, because wherever he was, he was always found faithful.

I.   Faithful as a <u>Son</u>

It all started with Israel (formerly Jacob) and Rachel. It was with his parents that Joseph began his preparation and training that ultimately allowed him to save both his own family and his people.

Illustration (poem, "Walk a Little Plainer, Daddy")

"Walk a little plainer, daddy"
Said a little boy so frail
"I'm following in your footsteps
And I don't want to fail

"Sometimes your steps are very plain
Sometimes they are so hard to see
So walk a little plainer, daddy
For you are leading me.

"I know that once you walked this way
Many years ago
And what you did along the way
I'd really like to know

"For sometimes when I am tempted
I don't know what to do
So walk a little plainer, daddy
For I must follow you.

"Someday when I'm grown up
You are like I want to be
Then I will have a little boy
Who will want to follow me

And I would want to lead him right
And help him to be true
So walk a little plainer, daddy
For we must follow you." (Author Unknown)

176

Illustration (Sons of Robert E Lee)

George Washington Custis Lee ("Custis"); 1832–1913; graduated first in his class, West Point 1854; served as Major General in the Confederate Army and aide-de-camp to President Jefferson Davis

William Henry Fitzhugh Lee ("Rooney"); 1837–1891; served as Major General in the Confederate Army (cavalry); severely wounded in battle at Culpepper, Virginia

Robert Edward Lee, Jr. (Rob); 1843–1914; served as Captain in the Confederate Army (Rockbridge Artillery)

Illustration (Sons of Theodore Roosevelt)

After the United States entered the World War I in 1917, former President Theodore Roosevelt asked the current President Woodrow Wilson for permission to raise a division of troops to fight in France. Wilson refused the request. "Forbidden to go himself, (Roosevelt) felt supreme satisfaction in the going of all his four sons.... They did honor to the Roosevelt name. Theodore, Jr., became a Lieutenant-Colonel, Kermit and Archibald became Captains; and Quentin, the youngest, a Lieutenant of Aviation, was killed in an air battle." (Theodore Roosevelt; An Intimate Biography, by William Roscoe Thayer)

   Theodore Roosevelt, Jr.—For his service in World War I, he won the Silver Star and the Distinguished Service Cross. A brigadier general during World War II, he won the Medal of Honor for his actions on D-Day (June 6, 1944), when he led troops ashore at Utah Beach, in France. He died of a heart attack in France on July 12, 1944. (information from World Book Encyclopedia)

A. LOVED BY HIS FATHER

GENESIS 37:3

3   Now Israel loved Joseph more than all his children, because he was the son of his old age: and he made him a coat of many colours.

It is well-known that Joseph was his father's favorite. It is imperative for believers today to know that God not only loves the world as a whole, but that He loves us individually. God wants to do special things for each and every one of us as well. Just as Joseph was loved by his earthly father, we too are loved by our Heavenly Father.

B. HATED BY HIS BROTHERS

GENESIS 37:4

4   *And when his brethren saw that their father loved him more than all his brethren, they hated him, and could not speak peaceably unto him.*

Joseph had a great burden in his life, and that was his unpleasant relationship with his brothers. Jealousy was their problem, just as it is a problem in many families today. The Word of God says that his brothers hated Joseph to the point that they could not speak even peaceably to him (Genesis 37:4). It is a beautiful picture for believers today to realize that, while many will not accept us or be happy with us, our Father still loves us and can still use us.

C. OBEDIENT TO HIS CALL

GENESIS 37:14

14   *And he* [Joseph's father Israel] *said to him, Go, I pray thee, see whether it be well with thy brethren, and well with the flocks; and bring me word again. So he sent him out of the vale of Hebron, and he came to Shechem.*

One of the great lessons of Joseph's life was that he obeyed his father even when the commands could not have been comfortable or enjoyable. His father sent him to his brothers who, as we have already learned, hated him. Joseph simply obeyed. Our Heavenly Father has sent us to evangelize a world which sometimes hates us. But it is simply our job to obey.

Lesson Twelve—Joseph—Living Like Jesus

II. Faithful as a <u>Servant</u>

Joseph's brothers wanted to get rid of him; through a series of circumstances, Joseph was sold as a slave and taken to Egypt. He had been faithful as a son, and it seemed that all it brought him was persecution. Now he would prove that he would be faithful in the role of a servant as well.

There is always a job for those who are willing to serve. The greatest example of a servant is the Lord Jesus Christ. It was said about our Saviour, that He came not to be ministered unto, but to minister and to give His life (Mark 10:45). Everywhere Joseph went, he was willing to serve. His willingness to serve brought him into leadership and, ultimately, opportunity. It is very important to note that God raises up and God puts down. In Potiphar's house (Genesis 39:2) and in the prison (Genesis 39:21), we see that it is clearly stated that "the LORD was with Joseph."

MATTHEW 23:11

11 But he that is greatest among you shall be your servant.

Illustration

When we reach Heaven, it won't matter what our title, our position, or our social or economic standing was here on Earth. Our Lord's highest praise will be, "Well done, thou good and faithful servant: thou hast been faithful over a few things, I will make thee ruler over many things: enter thou into the joy of thy lord" (Matthew 25:21, 23).

A. POTIPHAR'S HOUSE

Joseph became a servant in the house of Potiphar, a prominent man in Egypt who was an officer of Pharaoh and captain of the guard. Potiphar saw Joseph's faithfulness and grew to trust him implicitly.

GENESIS 39:4

4 And Joseph found grace in his sight, and he served him: and he made him overseer over his house, and all that he had he put into his hand.

Such trust is a valuable gift and should never be taken lightly.

PROVERBS 22:1

1   A good name is rather to be chosen than great riches, and loving favour rather than silver and gold.

In the first of several uncomfortable positions, Joseph was willing to serve. There is no doubt that a cantankerous, lazy man would not have been made overseer of Potiphar's house. Joseph did not grow bitter at his terrible situation: he decided to serve, faithfully and diligently.

B. PHARAOH'S PRISON

Potiphar's wife also appreciated Joseph, but for a different and unsavory reason. She tried to seduce him, but Joseph refused her and said, "…how then can I do this great wickedness, and sin against God?" (Genesis 39:9). She wouldn't give up, kept after him, and finally one day when they were all alone she physically grabbed him. He was forced to run away, leaving his garment in her hand. She looked at it and saw her opportunity to get even. She claimed he had tried to rape her and got him thrown into prison. So again, Joseph was in trouble through no fault of his own. How would he react? This time, he was faithful as a prisoner—and so faithful that he was virtually put in charge of the prison!

GENESIS 39:21–22

21   But the LORD was with Joseph, and shewed him mercy, and gave him favour in the sight of the keeper of the prison.
22   And the keeper of the prison committed to Joseph's hand all the prisoners that were in the prison; and whatsoever they did there, he was the doer of it.

Being lied about and mistreated did not stop Joseph from receiving God's favor or from serving his Lord. Admittedly, being lied about can be very painful, but a faithful Christian must learn to accept mistreatment, unfairness, and misunderstanding.

Lesson Twelve—Joseph—Living Like Jesus

ROMANS 8:35

35   Who shall separate us from the love of Christ? shall tribulation, or distress, or persecution, or famine, or nakedness, or peril, or sword?

2 TIMOTHY 3:12

12   Yea, and all that will live godly in Christ Jesus shall suffer persecution.

JOHN 16:33

33   These things I have spoken unto you, that in me ye might have peace. In the world ye shall have tribulation: but be of good cheer; I have overcome the world.

Often times, all that it takes to stop people from serving God is for others to lie about them. This was not true of Joseph: he was always faithful.

C. PEOPLE OF EGYPT

After being marooned in prison for years, Joseph remained faithful and, ultimately, was made prime minister over the entire country of Egypt. He had been given the opportunity to show Pharaoh that he had true wisdom from God, and Pharaoh knew that Joseph was the man to help him rule his nation.

GENESIS 41:38–44

38   And Pharaoh said unto his servants, Can we find such a one as this is, a man in whom the Spirit of God is?

39   And Pharaoh said unto Joseph, Forasmuch as God hath shewed thee all this, there is none so discreet and wise as thou art:

40   Thou shalt be over my house, and according unto thy word shall all my people be ruled: only in the throne will I be greater than thou.

41   And Pharaoh said unto Joseph, See, I have set thee over all the land of Egypt.

42   And Pharaoh took off his ring from his hand, and put it upon Joseph's hand, and arrayed him in vestures of fine linen, and put a gold chain about his neck;

181

43   And he made him to ride in the second chariot which he had; and they cried before him, Bow the knee: and he made him ruler over all the land of Egypt.

44   And Pharaoh said unto Joseph, I am Pharaoh, and without thee shall no man lift up his hand or foot in all the land of Egypt.

Joseph had a lot of ups and downs in his life: from his father's favorite son to a slave in a foreign land, from a trusted servant to a disgraced prisoner to a prison trustee, and now to second in command of the nation of Egypt. To Joseph, this was another opportunity to serve.

God's ways are not our ways, and God's timing is not always our timing. But as the psalmist urged, we sometimes need to simply wait on the Lord.

PSALM 27:14

14   Wait on the LORD: be of good courage, and he shall strengthen thine heart: wait, I say, on the LORD.

III.   Faithful as a Sovereign

The final stage of Joseph's life was spent as a sovereign. Even in this role, he foreshadowed the coming Messiah. Like the Lord Jesus Christ, he was rejected by his brethren, imprisoned, and mistreated, but after it all he also emerged victorious.

Illustration (Positional Increases)

Almost everyone has heard of John Deere. You've seen the name on farm, forestry, construction, and lawn equipment. You don't even need to see the name because you will probably recognize the familiar green and yellow color scheme. For many years, the advertising slogan was "Nothing runs like a Deere." But John Deere himself—as developer of the world's first commercially successful, self-scouring steel plow—might have been just another footnote in history instead of one of the world's most famous brand names, had it not been for his son Charles. From the John Deere company website, we have this information: "With his education completed,

Lesson Twelve—Joseph—Living Like Jesus

Charles joined the company as a bookkeeper in 1853, at the age of 16. Working his way through a variety of positions, Charles quickly earned a reputation as a keen businessman. This must have delighted John, as it allowed the father and son to both focus on what they did best—Charles handling the business, and John attending to the products and sales….By 1858, John had turned over management of the business to Charles, who was just 21 at the time."

"Charles Deere was an outstanding businessman who established marketing centers, called branch houses, to serve the network of independent retail dealers. By the time of Charles Deere's death in 1907, the company was making a wide range of steel plows, cultivators, corn and cotton planters, and other implements." John Deere himself died in 1886, but "his legacy lived on in a way he could have never imagined. His descendents or their spouses went on to lead the company John Deere founded for the next 96 years."

A. Forgiving sovereign

In his position of Pharaoh's right-hand man and in charge of the food supply, Joseph one day received some visitors. Famine had come to the land of Canaan, and Israel sent his sons to Egypt because (thanks to Joseph's wisdom and planning) there was corn there. The brothers did not recognize this regal and imposing figure as the annoying little brother they thought they had rid themselves of years ago, but Joseph knew them. He had been at their mercy and they sought his destruction; now they were at his mercy and he had the same opportunity: if he had sent them away empty-handed, he would be consigning them to death by starvation. But in a beautiful story of mercy and forgiveness, Joseph took them in and met their needs abundantly.

Genesis 50:17–21

17   So shall ye say unto Joseph, Forgive, I pray thee now, the trespass of thy brethren, and their sin; for they did unto thee evil:

and now, we pray thee, forgive the trespass of the servants of the God of thy father. And Joseph wept when they spake unto him.

18 And his brethren also went and fell down before his face; and they said, Behold, we be thy servants.

19 And Joseph said unto them, Fear not: for am I in the place of God?

20 But as for you, ye thought evil against me; but God meant it unto good, to bring to pass, as it is this day, to save much people alive.

21 Now therefore fear ye not: I will nourish you, and your little ones. And he comforted them, and spake kindly unto them.

Once again we see a picture of Jesus in the life of Joseph. What do we sinners deserve from God but death and eternal separation? And yet...

ROMANS 5:8–10

8 But God commendeth his love toward us, in that, while we were yet sinners, Christ died for us.

9 Much more then, being now justified by his blood, we shall be saved from wrath through him.

10 For if, when we were enemies, we were reconciled to God by the death of his Son, much more, being reconciled, we shall be saved by his life.

EPHESIANS 4:32

32 And be ye kind one to another, tenderhearted, forgiving one another, even as God for Christ's sake hath forgiven you.

Joseph was willing to forgive the incredible injustices that had been visited upon him by his hateful brothers. One of the most beautiful lessons in all of the pages of Scripture is located in Genesis 50:19–21, where Joseph clearly states that he understood that judgment was of the Lord, and that his brothers were not to fear, for he would take care of them.

Human logic would have compelled Joseph to use his vast power to distribute to his brothers a just retribution for their mean and evil acts toward him, but Joseph did not conduct himself according to human logic, nor was he a slave to his emotions. Joseph reacted with love, mercy and true justice. He would allow God to deliver retribution as He saw fit. Joseph would not overstep his authority and take God's job into his own hands. Although the words would not be penned for many centuries, Joseph understood this truth:

ROMANS 12:19

19 *Dearly beloved, avenge not yourselves, but rather give place unto wrath: for it is written, Vengeance is mine; I will repay, saith the Lord.*

B. SAVING SOVEREIGN

GENESIS 50:20

20 *But as for you, ye thought evil against me; but God meant it unto good, to bring to pass, as it is this day, to save much people alive.*

Joseph realized that God had put him into a position to save his family and his people, and he decided that he would accept this responsibility with personal passion and fervent diligence.

Like the Lord has for us, Joseph had a place for his family, and he had a plan for them. He would not allow his family to go uncared for, unprotected, and unprovided for. Not only was it Joseph's immediate family who found salvation and blessing, but the nation of Israel itself was strengthened and brought into prominence because of Joseph. God used this man to minister to an entire nation. In our quest to be like our Saviour, by whose name we claim our very identity as Christians, it is easy to overlook many to whom God would have us minister. As you look for the return of Christ on the horizon, are you overlooking those to whom He desires you to minister at this moment? Be very cautious that, in your impatience for His return, you do not overlook the mission you have now.

Conclusion

Faithfulness. If one word would be used to describe the life of Joseph, it would without a doubt be the word *faithfulness*. In every situation into which he was plunged, thrown, or placed, Joseph was completely faithful: he was dedicated to his cause and to his testimony and the testimony of God. How dedicated are you? How faithful are you to the name of the Lord and to the calling and responsibility He has placed in your life? Perhaps it's time you allowed yourself to accept the truths of the life of Joseph as if you had never heard them before. Do not be afraid to let them affect you. Do not be afraid to let the truths of God's Word change who you are. And do not be afraid to stand up and live for Christ!

Lesson Twelve—Joseph—Living Like Jesus

Study Questions

1. Why was Joseph so loved by his father and hated by his brothers?
    His father loved Joseph because he was the son of his old age. His brothers hated Joseph because of jealousy: they saw that he was their father's favorite.

2. What did Joseph do that was the "last straw" for his brothers?
    He obeyed his father by checking up on them.

3. How did Potiphar show that he trusted Joseph?
    He put Joseph in charge of the house and all that he had.

4. How did Joseph end up in prison in Egypt?
    Potiphar's wife lied about him and said that he had tried to rape her.

5. Describe a time in your life when you were misunderstood and lied about, and how you reacted to it.
    Answers will vary.

6. When Joseph got out of prison, what was his new position?
    Pharaoh made him his second-in-command, his prime minister, and put him in charge of the food supply.

7. Describe how God has brought blessing into your life through circumstances you did not understand.
    Answers will vary.

8. Although they may not deserve it, whom will you forgive this week?
    Answers will vary.

187

Memory Verse

And we know that all things work together for good to them that love God, to them who are the called according to his purpose.
—ROMANS 8:28

LESSON THIRTEEN

JONATHAN
True Friendship

Text

1 SAMUEL 18:1–4

1   *And it came to pass, when he had made an end of speaking unto Saul, that the soul of Jonathan was knit with the soul of David, and Jonathan loved him as his own soul.*

2   *And Saul took him that day, and would let him go no more home to his father's house.*

3   *Then Jonathan and David made a covenant, because he loved him as his own soul.*

4   *And Jonathan stripped himself of the robe that was upon him, and gave it to David, and his garments, even to his sword, and to his bow, and to his girdle.*

Overview

Jonathan was David's best friend in the years before David became king, and he was just the type of friend David needed at the time. In this lesson we'll take a look at how Jonathan strengthened David when he was weak, how he gave to David when he was in need, and how he warned David when he was in danger. These things he did selflessly, and so his example has come down to us as the epitome of what a friend should be.

Lesson Theme

A true friend is a precious gift from God. But as blessed as it is to have a friend, it is a greater blessing to be a friend. As we study the relationship of Jonathan and David, let's take the challenge to be a better friend to our friends.

189

Lesson Goals

At the conclusion of the lesson, each student should:

1. Understand the personal qualities of Jonathan that made him a good example of a friend
2. Understand the effects of Jonathan's friendship on the life of David
3. Determine to emulate the qualities of Jonathan as a friend

Teaching Outline

Introduction

    I. Strengthening Friendship
        A. Sought David physically
        B. Strengthened David spiritually

    II. Giving Friendship
        A. Gave his possessions
        B. Gave his position
        C. Gave his promise

    III. Warning Friendship
        A. Timely
        B. Trusted

Conclusion

LESSON THIRTEEN

JONATHAN
True Friendship

Text

1 SAMUEL 18:1–4

1   And it came to pass, when he had made an end of speaking unto Saul, that the soul of Jonathan was knit with the soul of David, and Jonathan loved him as his own soul.

2   And Saul took him that day, and would let him go no more home to his father's house.

3   Then Jonathan and David made a covenant, because he loved him as his own soul.

4   And Jonathan stripped himself of the robe that was upon him, and gave it to David, and his garments, even to his sword, and to his bow, and to his girdle.

Introduction

Jesus is a friend who sticks closer than a brother. As the songwriter said, "No one ever cared for me like Jesus." This can be a lonely world, and people here are hungry for true friendship. An examination of Jonathan's life will reveal several attributes that should be a part of every good friendship.

I. Strengthening Friendship

In the world today, most people view a friendship as a relationship from which they can gain something. Jonathan's life, however, typified a friendship that was characterized by giving rather than receiving. Jonathan gave strength to David at a time when he needed strength. Two friends standing together should be stronger than either one could be alone. Friends strengthen each other: when one is weak, the other needs to help hold him up. Think of Aaron and Hur holding up the hands of Moses and thus helping Israel win the battle against the Amalekites (Exodus 17:8–13). As we fight the battles of life, we so much appreciate those friends who stand by us.

PROVERBS 17:17
17 *A friend loveth at all times, and a brother is born for adversity.*

Illustration (Portion of a letter from John Wesley to William Wilberforce, dated February 26, 1791)

For years William Wilberforce had pushed in Britain's Parliament for the abolition of slavery. Discouraged, he was about to give up. His elderly friend, John Wesley, heard of it and wrote a short note of encouragement:

"Unless the divine power has raised you up... I see not how you can go through your glorious enterprise, in opposing that execrable villany, which is the scandal of religion, of England, and of human nature. Unless God has raised you up for this very thing, you will be worn-out by the opposition of men and devils. But, if God be for you, who can be against you? Are all of them together stronger than God? O be not weary in well doing! Go on; in the name of God and in the power of His might, till even American slavery (the vilest that ever saw the sun) shall vanish away before it."

John Wesley died just a few days later; the final abolition of slavery in the British Empire was more than forty years in

Lesson Thirteen—Jonathan—True Friendship

the future, but with renewed faith Wilberforce would continue the struggle.

Illustration

The Sequoia trees of California tower as much as 300 feet above the ground. Strangely, these giants have unusually shallow root systems that reach out in all directions to capture the greatest amount of surface moisture. Seldom will you see a redwood standing alone because high winds would quickly uproot it. That's why they grow in clusters. Their intertwining roots provide support for one another against the storms. (Fredericksburg Bible Illustrator Supplements)

A. Sought David physically

1 Samuel 23:16

16 *And Jonathan Saul's son arose, and went to David into the wood,* and strengthened his hand in God.

Jonathan went to David to be a friend to him and to help him. When David was in hiding from the relentless pursuit of the jealous King Saul, Jonathan took the time and invested the effort to find him and go to him. It is not always easy and convenient to go to people in need, but it is always right. Yes, we are all busy, but we should never be too busy to help someone in need—whatever that need might be. The Bible gives other illustrations of deliberately seeking someone out in order to help and be a friend: Andrew went to Peter to bring him to Christ (John 1:40–42). Philip went to the Ethiopian eunuch to give him the Gospel (Acts 8:26–39). Jesus said that there would be great rewards in eternity for those Christians who took the time to minister "unto the least of these" (Matthew 25:31–40). It has been said that you can impress from a distance, but you can only impact from up close. In the parable of the lost sheep, Christ told how the shepherd loved that one sheep enough to leave the ninety-nine in the wilderness to seek and go to the one that needed help.

193

B. Strengthened David spiritually

1 Samuel 23:16

16   *And Jonathan Saul's son arose, and went to David into the wood, and* **strengthened his hand in God.**

It is good to feed people; it is good to clothe people; and it is good to encourage people. But how much more important it is to strengthen someone in the Lord! Hebrews 11 gives us a long list of people whom God honored because they sought to strengthen others spiritually.

II. Giving Friendship

It could be said that love can be spelled "g-i-v-e." This could include the giving of time and it could be the sharing of material gifts, but there is no question that when we love someone, we desire to give to them. The world today is becoming increasingly selfish and materialistic. Christians should seek to be the exact opposite of this. We are to be like Christ and the Heavenly Father who gave. "For God so loved the world that he **gave**..." (John 3:16).

Illustration

If Barbie is so popular, why do you have to buy her friends?

Illustration (Associated Press, 2002)

TAMPA, Florida—With wads of cash strapped to his body and hoping to make some people happy, Kevin Shelton gave away $1 bills while strolling through a mall.

In two hours, Shelton says he gave away about $7,000—with only smiles and a few thank you's to show for it.

"It's what I choose to do," he said Friday after the cash giveaway. "I think it's making an impact."

Shelton, 32, says he earned his money buying and selling real estate in the Tampa Bay area.

Reactions at the International Plaza varied—from hugs to lectures for not giving the money to the poor.

Most shoppers happily took the free money and walked away giggling. Some vowed to give it away. Others planned to buy a lottery ticket.

Shelton began doling out cash last year as a way to brighten people's day and spark generosity. He swears it's not a gimmick. He says he doesn't keep track of what he gives away, but guesses it's in the tens of thousands.

Illustration

Have you ever heard the term "penny pincher," and the expression, "He can pinch a penny so thin you can see through it?"

Hetty Green was the extreme epitome of those words. For many years, she was called America's greatest miser. When she died in 1916, she left an estate valued at 100 million dollars, an especially vast fortune for that day, comparable to more than a billion today.

But in spite of all her vast wealth, Hetty was so miserly that she ate cold oatmeal in order to save the expense of heating the water. When her son had a severe leg injury, she took so long trying to find a free clinic to treat him that his leg had to be amputated because of advanced infection.

It has been said that Hetty hastened her own death by bringing on a seizure while arguing the merits of skim milk because it was cheaper than whole milk.

Although Hetty Green is an extreme example, many people have a miserly outlook on life. The lives of some people are cold and miserly, instead of demonstrating the warmth and generosity of God's love to those around them.

A. GAVE HIS POSSESSIONS

1 SAMUEL 18:3–4

3   Then Jonathan and David made a covenant, because he loved him as his own soul.

4   And Jonathan stripped himself of the robe that was upon him, and gave it to David, and his garments, even to his sword, and to his bow, and to his girdle.

It has been rightly said that something is not **real** until it is **personal**. Jonathan was willing to give of his personal goods to help his friend. He gave his clothing, and he gave his armaments. He gave things of real value. He gave things which he certainly used and about which he deeply cared. There is no question that this sent a message of love and sincere friendship to David.

B. Gave his <u>position</u>

1 Samuel 23:17

17 And he said unto him, Fear not: for the hand of Saul my father shall not find thee; and thou shalt be king over Israel, and I shall be next unto thee; and that also Saul my father knoweth.

Jonathan was the heir to the throne of Israel, but he knew that David was God's man for that time. He was willing to step aside graciously from his own honorable position in order that God could be glorified. God's Word plainly teaches that the first shall be last and the last first (Matthew 19:28–30). Now, three thousand years later, we are still discussing and learning from a man who was not greedily grasping for his own promotion, but was rather attempting to promote his friend.

C. Gave his <u>promise</u>

1 Samuel 20:4

4 Then said Jonathan unto David, Whatsoever thy soul desireth, I will even do it for thee.

It is interesting that Jonathan gave not only in the present moment, but he promised to help fulfill future needs. The challenging truth of this passage is that Jonathan's desire to aid his friend had no boundaries. He said, "whatsoever thy soul desireth, I will do it...." There was no limitation on what Jonathan would attempt to do for his friend David.

Lesson Thirteen—Jonathan—True Friendship

III. <u>Warning Friendship</u>

While true friends will give and strengthen, true friends will also warn. A warning given in a timely manner can greatly help a friend. David needed to know what Saul's intentions were toward him, and Jonathan undertook great personal risk to communicate with him.

Friendship is so much more than just two people who enjoy spending time together. A real friend is willing to "stick his neck out." A real friend will courageously tell the truth when it isn't easy. A real friend will do what it takes to be sure that no harm comes to his friend. We would all like to have this kind of friend. Are you willing to **be** this kind of friend?

Illustration (Burma Shave signs)

> Trains don't wander
> All over the map
> 'Cause nobody sits
> In the engineer's lap
> —Burma Shave

> She kissed the hairbrush
> By mistake
> She thought it was
> Her husband Jake
> —Burma Shave

Remember these? For those who never saw any of the Burma Shave signs, here is a quick lesson in our history of the 1930s and '40s. Before there were interstates, when everyone drove the old two-lane roads, Burma Shave signs would be posted all over the countryside in farmers' fields. They were small red signs with white letters. Five signs, about 100 feet apart, and each contained 1 line of a 4-line couplet... and the obligatory fifth sign advertising Burma Shave, a popular shaving cream. (Submitted by Nancy A. Thomas to www.witandwisdom.org)

Here are more of the actual signs:

197

Lessons from Legends

Don't lose your head
To gain a minute
You need your head
Your brains are in it
—Burma Shave

Drove too long
Driver snoozing
What happened next
Is not amusing
—Burma Shave

Brother speeder
Let's rehearse
All together
Good morning, nurse
—Burma Shave

Speed was high
Weather was not
Tires were thin
X marks the spot
—Burma Shave

No matter the price
No matter how new
The best safety device
In the car is you
—Burma Shave

A guy who drives
A car wide open
Is not thinkin'
He's just hopin'
—Burma Shave

At intersections
Look each way
A harp sounds nice
But it's hard to play
—Burma Shave

Lesson Thirteen—Jonathan—True Friendship

Both hands on the wheel
Eyes on the road
That's the skillful
Driver's code
—Burma Shave

The one who drives
When he's been drinking
Depends on you
To do his thinking
—Burma Shave

And my all-time favorite:
Passing school zone
Take it slow
Let our little
Shavers grow
—Burma Shave

Illustration

The Winter 1991 issue of the UNIVERSITY OF PACIFIC REVIEW offered a chilling description of the 1986 Chernobyl (Soviet Union) nuclear disaster: "There were two electrical engineers in the control room that night, and the best thing that could be said for what they were doing is that they were 'playing around' with the machine. They were performing what the Soviets later described as an unauthorized experiment. They were trying to see how long a turbine would 'free wheel' when they took the power off it.

"Now, taking power off that kind of a nuclear reactor is a difficult, dangerous thing to do, because these reactors are very unstable in their lower ranges. In order to get the reactor down to that kind of power, where they could perform the test they were interested in performing, they had to override manually six separate computer-driven alarm systems. One by one the computers would come up and say, 'Stop, Dangerous! Go no further!' And one by one, rather than shutting off the experiment, they shut off the alarms and kept going. You know the results:

199

nuclear fallout that was recorded all around the world, from the largest industrial accident ever to occur in the world."

The instructions and warnings in Scripture are just as clear as the computers of Chernobyl. We ignore them at our own peril, and tragically, at the peril of others. (Tom Tripp, from *Leadership*)

A. Timely

1 Samuel 20:19–22

19   And when thou hast stayed three days, then thou shalt go down quickly, and come to the place where thou didst hide thyself when the business was in hand, and shalt remain by the stone Ezel.

20   And I will shoot three arrows on the side thereof, as though I shot at a mark.

21   And, behold, I will send a lad, saying, Go, find out the arrows. If I expressly say unto the lad, Behold, the arrows are on this side of thee, take them; then come thou: for there is peace to thee, and no hurt; as the Lord liveth.

22   But if I say thus unto the young man, Behold, the arrows are beyond thee; go thy way: for the Lord hath sent thee away.

Jonathan let David know what he needed to do at the exact moment he needed it. Jonathan wanted to protect his friend; he wanted to help him; he wanted to encourage him. Even though it was hard for Jonathan, he went to great effort to make sure that David received the necessary warning in a timely manner. Procrastination at this point in David's journey may have cost him his life, and Jonathan was willing to give anything and everything that would help him.

B. Trusted

In the Old Testament, angels came to Lot and told him of Sodom's coming destruction (Genesis 19). When he shared this news with his sons-in-law, his warning was disregarded because of his own poor testimony, and he was mocked (Genesis 19:14). On the other hand, when David received

Lesson Thirteen—Jonathan—True Friendship

Jonathan's warning, he responded with complete trust. Ultimately, David was rescued because of Jonathan's warning. It is important to realize that our testimonies can greatly affect how people receive our message.

Conclusion

Friendship is important. Friends have influence. Jonathan realized this and sought to use his influence in a way that would encourage and sharpen David. Would to God that we would be as good a friend to those around us as Jonathan was to David. Jonathan was a strengthening friend, a giving friend, and a warning friend. He valued the heart and life of David more than he did his own personal comfort. Are you this kind of friend?

Lessons from Legends

Study Questions

1. What was Jonathan's position in the kingdom of Saul?
    He was Saul's oldest son and heir to the throne.

2. What does the Bible say about Jonathan's friendship for David at the very start of their relationship?
    The Bible says that "the soul of Jonathan was knit with the soul of David, and Jonathan loved him as his own soul."

3. Where was David when Jonathan went to strengthen his hand in God?
    David was in the wood, hiding from Saul.

4. What did Jonathan give to David in order to show his friendship?
    Jonathan gave David his possessions (his robe, garments, sword, and bow), his position (stepped aside because he knew that God had chosen David as successor to Saul), and his promise (anything David needed or wanted, Jonathan would see that he got it).

5. What was the warning that Jonathan gave David?
    Jonathan warned David that Saul was coming after him and he needed to get away.

6. What can you do strengthen a friend's hand in God this week?
    Answers will vary.

7. What can you do to meet the needs of a friend this week?
    Answers will vary.

202

Lesson Thirteen—Jonathan—True Friendship

8. If you have a friend who is headed for trouble, will you be the one to give a loving warning?
   Answers will vary.

Memory Verse

And Jonathan Saul's son arose, and went to David into the wood, and strengthened his hand in God.—1 SAMUEL 23:16

For additional Christian
growth resources visit
www.strivingtogether.com